WHERE DOES THIS ROAD GO?

WHERE DOES THIS ROAD GO?

A Boomer's Walkabout

MARTIN H. CROWE

Moving River Press

Moving River Press

Kingston, MA

ISBN-10: 0615859313

ISBN-13: 9780615859316

For Remlee, Amber, and Cooper

Who brighten the future

Acknowledgements

I was not sure what I would find when I set out on my walkabout. The only certainty was that my family and friends would play a big role, as they always have in my life. Many of them appear in this book by first name only. Last names were omitted to avoid asking so many people if I represented their thoughts accurately! So, I take full responsibility for remembering (or not) what they were truly trying to say to me.

All of the family and friends mentioned in the book played a large role in keeping me honest about everything I was saying and doing. Some of them went above and beyond mere friendship by editing and commenting on various drafts of the book. Becky Wells helped me accept that it was okay for readers to laugh, cry, and shake their heads with curiosity about where the story was going. Her questions helped me understand what was missing.

My brother, Rodger Crowe, was relentless with his red pen, for all things grammatical, and hammered away at the sense of things, until I understood why a paragraph had to be rewritten. Fortunately, he has learned considerable tact since we wrestled and tumbled as smart-mouthed kids (OK, so I was the one with the smart mouth!) My sister, Kathy Anderson, worked for me for several years editing training materials and still uses as many yellow tabs to mark my transgressions. Her attention to detail on multiple levels swept away innumerable inconsistencies. She also has a talent for finding paragraphs that deserve a better home in the manuscript.

All three of my children played a large role in my walkabout by their interest and conversations with me about the process. Remlee did major editing and helped me understand the links between places, ideas, and the point of talking about something or not. Her questions illuminated a few murky areas that needed fixing. She is not one to suffer fools gladly, and made no exceptions for me! Amber got rid of many of my words that were repetitive, boring, or just downright inadequate. Her suggestions for expansion or deletion were just too good to ignore. Cooper did a much faster job of adapting to a new life in college than I did adapting to a new life without daily responsibilities. We had several long trips together during the walkabout that allowed us to trade stories about the huge shift in our lives.

The last reviewer, Linda Paquette, had the advantage of reading a later revision of the manuscript. Nonetheless, she found multiple ways of improving it. Her questions forced me to commit to what I was writing and stand by my words.

In addition to the written feedback all the reviewers provided me, we had multiple conversations about the flow of the book and the book title. Asking people for their opinions is risky, particularly if they all hold nothing back. So this is a better book than I could have achieved alone.

I also want to thank all the friends and family who provided me food, shelter, enjoyment and a sounding board, as I pursued my walkabout. There were a few strangers I met along the road who played a part in my thinking as well. Finally, I want to thank Tex and O.B. (Jim Palermo and Denis O'Brien) for encouraging me for many years to share my writing with others.

CONTENTS

Acknowledgements vii

Introduction 1

1. Base Camp 13

2. Repack/Reload 39

3. Rhythm of the Road 51

4. Head for Water . . . . ·79

5. Sit and Ponder 105

6. Camping Out 121

7. Turnaround 139

8. Cotton Fields Forever 149

9. Old Guys Napping 155

10. Heading Home 169

11. Fog Of Politics 193

12. Last Night of My Walkabout 211

13. Commit to Purpose 219

Afterword 229

A Boomer's Walkabout

INTRODUCTION

It seemed like a good idea at the time. Why not start thinking about my future as a retired 65 year old, now that my son's college decision had been made? It was several weeks before his high school graduation. All the decisions had been made and we knew where and when he was going to college. He was staying at a friend's house that night and I thought, what the heck, may as well start thinking about what my future might look like. This was a really bad idea.

Within two minutes, I was in a panic. Everything that came to mind spiraled me further out of control. You're going to be alone. No one else lives here in this big four-bedroom house. You have nothing to get you out of bed in the morning. Your phone will stop ringing. You're too old to get a job. Who's going to hire a 65 year old? You know you hate selling your services as a training consultant. How can you afford this house in Kingston, Massachusetts and college bills?

Awooga, ring, ring, put that firewall back up! No more thinking. I can't get there from here. I need a different path.

I'm not sure when it first occurred to me to take a walkabout. For several years, I had it in the back of my mind that my life would change dramatically when my son, Cooper, would graduate from high school. My wife, Kitty, had passed away in February 2005, of gall bladder cancer. Our two daughters had both moved back home during the year that their mother battled her illness. But, both were now off in their own places, pursuing their own relationships and careers.

My only acknowledgement of this upcoming change was in emails I sent during a brief attempt at online dating in 2010, where I said something like both my son and I will be facing a new horizon soon. I still made no effort to think about my new horizon. It was far more interesting to help guide my son through the myriad choices of targeting colleges, visiting them, making a final selection, working on applications, essays, interviews, and so on. Plus, the intricacies of financial aid forms carry their own form of torment, while also eating up your time.

When friends or family asked me what I was going to do after Cooper went off to college, I blithely told them I'd figure it out then. When they made suggestions to go back to volunteering in youth sports or work at a food pantry, I nodded politely and said, "Yep, there are a lot of things out there to do." Inwardly, I'm saying "Been there, done that!" I coached and helped run youth sports organizations for over 30 years. It was all fun because my kids were there and it made a difference in their lives. I loved it while I was doing it, but I think it would feel very different if I was not benefiting my own children during the hundreds of hours a year it would take. I felt that I had done my part and it was now time for other parents to step up and be a positive role model. I also did the food pantry work, too, and I could not see that becoming the focus of my life; an interest, perhaps, but not the focus.

I was not looking to fill up my time. I had already done that for many years. I knew how to survive, but I wanted to learn to thrive again. I was looking to make a new life. A life that was as challenging, exciting, and fun-filled as the one I had enjoyed before. My life changed dramatically when my wife passed away, but the core infrastructure of being a parent was still there. With my son off to college and my daughters living on their own, I still have opportunities as a parent (some call them obligations, but I always look at them as opportunities). But, the daily opportunities to be a part of their lives and the logistics of eating, transportation, and school support would no longer be there.

So, after almost forty years of building my life around what the family and children needed, I would go to bed each night and wake up each morning thinking about something other than family needs. What in the world was that going to be?

If I was going to live a different life, it seemed best to seek that out in a different place and not be constrained by old habits and daily routines. Quite a few years ago, I came across the concept of a walkabout. I think I first read about it in the book *Thorn Birds* by Colleen McCullough. Walkabouts were a traditional rite of adolescent passage among aborigines in Australia. Over time, the concept seemed to expand to include anyone who set aside his or her responsibilities and headed out into the world to find something new to focus on. There was also a passing reference to walkabouts in the movie *Crocodile Dundee*.

In any event, a walkabout, a little known word, had some appeal to describe an undertaking that no one else I had ever known attempted. The word was a more intriguing description than saying I was driving around and visiting family and friends and figuring out my future. More succinct, too! It also invited conversation.

One advantage of planning a walkabout is that it needed no plan. The mission was to find a mission, not get to a destination. It didn't matter where I went, so long as I left my comfort zone.

At first, I started writing down names of people I could visit along my walkabout. Talking with friends and family about my opportunity to build a new infrastructure for my life and find new purposes seemed a reasonable thing to do. While this began to set a pattern for my journey, it quickly became evident that I would be racing from one location to another, staying for two days in each place before driving 4-6 hours to get to the next place. Too many people, too many places meant little time for stopping and exploring or even much time to think seriously about anything.

So, I tossed aside the list of people and made a short list of places I wanted to spend more time in. Several places could be places to live in retirement, while others were interesting spots to visit. Each location had a few people nearby that I knew had the type of personality and outlook that would be challenging, forceful, energizing, and supportive of my wrestling with my future. Things I say in my own mind take on a different character when exposed to the conversational volley of other people. If you want to get better at tennis, you have to play with people of equal or greater skill. In a friendly yet competitive game, an easy lob can have as much impact as a hard smash. The people I planned to see knew this and were willing to do both as needed. Based on past experience, I knew these people were quite capable of making me think harder about what I was saying. No one was going to smile and say that sounds nice, when they were really thinking, "man, he's got no clue what he's talking about."

I began to think of the walkabout as an open-ended three months away from home, from September 1 to Thanksgiving. Three months with no timetable or interruptions. Nice idea - not gonna happen! The first obstacle that presented itself was my son's Fall Break from his college schedule. He would be home for a week in October. It is difficult, if not impossible, for me to pass up opportunities to be with any of my children. So, despite my intention to actually focus on myself for a while, there was no way I was going to miss his first visit home after living away from family for the first extended time.

There was also the little matter of Parent's Weekend at college, which was the third weekend of September. I briefly thought of skipping it, until my oldest daughter, Remlee, called to say she had booked us a hotel for the weekend. OK, so right away, the notion of an uninterrupted walkabout for three months was unraveling. Before my walkabout got close to beginning, it was time to go back to square one. Where to next?

The timetable for a walkabout got shredded pretty quickly, so I focused the first two weeks of August on helping Cooper pull together his clothes, supplies, and other gear to go off to college. Amber, my middle child, and her boyfriend, John, threw a going away party at her apartment for Cooper. Some of Amber and John's friends that Cooper had gotten to know were there, along with several of Cooper's friends. As I watched all these young people (from 18 to 40), I thought of how different things were since I had headed off to college. When I headed off to college in the sixties, I took one suitcase and a laundry bag with sheets and two notebooks. Like his two sisters before him, Cooper would be heading off with far more gear than I did.

In mid-August, Cooper, Remlee and I headed south to Philadelphia in a mid-sized car with the trunk stuffed. On top of the car was a storage bag that looked like the landing pad for stunt men falling off a ten-story building. In the rear seat, Cooper had to rest his arm on the computer he had built when he was fifteen years old. Wisely, they had purchased things at Bed, Bath and Beyond and arranged to pick them up at a store near campus.

Since we stayed at a motel the night before moving into the dorm, we had to take the storage bag into the hotel room to safeguard it. Fortunately, it was a first floor room, so we didn't have to wrestle it into an elevator and risk setting off an overload alarm. We had heard stories of move-in day elves at this college, which I frankly thought were shamelessly used as a recruiting tool. Lo and behold, the elves did show up at our arrival on campus on Friday and picked our car clean of anything not screwed down.

All the elves had disappeared when we returned the next day with another carload of stuff from Bed, Bath and Beyond, some storage drawers, and a few essentials from the grocery store. What college student starts off with less than a hundred dollars worth of soda pop, water, Gatorade, pretzels, chips, Cheezits, Goldfish, and salt and vinegar Pringles?

There were a couple of orientation events just for family on Friday and Saturday, while the students were getting their first dose of information they instinctively knew they were never going to need to know.

By 6:45 Saturday evening, it was time to say our good-byes. As we walked across the parking lot, I spied a large SUV with a trailer behind it and realized that was the exact rig we would need to get all his gear home for the summer. I also planned out the things I wanted to say to Cooper before I gave him a hug and a kiss – a last few words of advice, how proud I was of him, a few things to look out for, etc. I managed the hug and the kiss fine. The last few words swelled my chest and throat and stuck there – the same place they stuck when I dropped my two daughters off for their freshman year of college.

I did not really expect the third time to be any easier than the first two. All three times were different, yet the same. I hadn't learned much about doing this gracefully. So, I was glad that Remlee was driving as we left and waved goodbye to Cooper. The roadways were a little tricky, so I had to control my tears and help with directions.

There were a few other noteworthy events on the weekend. As if dropping Cooper off at his new home 350 miles away wasn't traumatic enough, there had been plenty of fire and brimstone. Thursday night when we went out to eat, there was a huge storm. Thunder, lightning, hail and torrential rains caused us to pull off the road and sit in a parking lot for 15 minutes before we could see enough to drive again. On Friday, when Remlee and I returned to our motel, there were flashing lights and stopped traffic on the

Interstate just after our exit. When we stopped for gas, we found out the Interstate had been closed for two hours in both directions due to a tanker truck leaking an unknown substance. Someone said the area was being evacuated. Everybody was asking for directions around the mess, but the attendant didn't speak English well enough to help anybody. I am pretty sure he was sending people into the airport parking garage when they were asking how to drive to New Jersey.

Then, on Saturday night while driving back on the Garden State Parkway, we spied smoke ahead, then flames coming from a car in the travel lane to our right. Of course, no one in New Jersey would let us into the lane to our left. As people started seeing the flames, traffic slowed down and we could finally pull into the left lane. By this time, the flames were shooting twenty feet into the air and the car was completely engulfed. Metal and plastic were melting and dripping off the car in little rivers of flame.

As I pondered the gauntlet of lightning, hail, torrential rains, chemical spill, and firestorm we had run through, I started to say, "What..". Remlee immediately interrupted me and said, "Don't even ask!"

But we made it by the burning car safely and got home at 1:30 in the morning.

Remlee dropped me off at home and I had another bad moment as she drove off to her house. It hit me that I was also losing watching Cooper and Remlee having all their playful, loving supportive time together two or three times a week. And losing Amber joining them two or three times a month. A third era of change – mine with Cooper, Remlee and Amber's with Cooper, and mine watching my three kids be best friends.

I sat on the couch and stared into darkness for about half an hour. My youngest child was off on his next stage of life, one that he was totally prepared for. I was about to face up to my next stage of life. Was I ready for it?

The next three days alone at home were inordinately long. What was the next road for me? Would I find a new rhythm to my life?

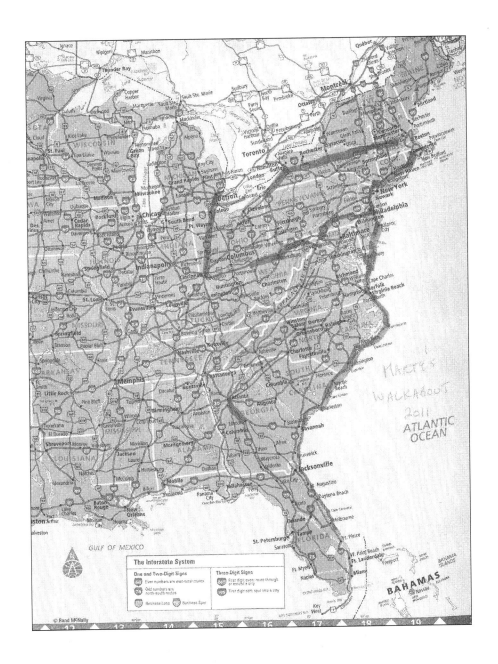

1. BASE CAMP

With my son off to college, I had three days to get ready for a visitor. Not that it required much preparation other than finding some pubs to listen to some Irish music and have a few pints of Guinness and Harp. My brother, Rodg, was coming back to New England for a visit. It was his first trip back to Boston since he moved away nine years ago to Cincinnati to be near his children and grandchildren.

Rodg's journey and mine dovetailed in a unique way. His journey was a journey of affirmation to overcome his qualms about traveling. After flying for over thirty years on both personal and business trips, he gradually developed a fear of heights. He decided to stop flying shortly after the 9/11 attacks, which confirmed his decision.

He was always a white-knuckle flier, but after 9/11, he decided to give up flying altogether. A six-hour car ride was about his limit for traveling alone. For a long-time traveler to Ireland, Europe, and many parts of the USA, the six-hour radius of opportunity finally became too limiting.

So, he decided to come back to Boston to see me, my kids, his friends in Portland, Maine, see the ocean, eat fresh seafood, and hear good Irish music. It took a six-hour car ride from Cincinnati to Erie, Pennsylvania (our hometown), to visit two of our sisters, a 14-hour train ride (which turned into 16) from Erie to Boston. Then, a 2.5-hour train ride from Boston to Portland, Maine and back again. Followed by a ten-hour car drive with me back to Erie and another 6-hour drive back home.

Overcoming the 900-mile barrier to seeing old friends, family, and familiar haunts took a considerable amount of planning. Moving beyond my constraints was a figurative goal for me, a literal one for Rodg.

Our time together turned into a base camp for me as we talked about the difference between his journey and mine. Much of our conversation was a testing ground for me to explore what I really meant about going on a walkabout and what I hoped to learn from it. Of course, we were up late sharing memories across the years from growing up on Rosedale Avenue in Erie and across the decades of our lives and careers. In an effort to understand him further, I even drank a glass of his sherry. I didn't learn anything significant from that, so I went back to my rum punch.

One day, we took a boat cruise around Plymouth Harbor and learned that Truman Capote once stayed on Clark's Island, which I see every day from my house above the harbor. Apparently, he wrote part of his best-seller book, *In Cold Blood*, there. Or, perhaps it was *Breakfast at Tiffany's*, according to other accounts. Our tour guide was a little fast and loose with the details.

The island was initially considered for the location of the Pilgrim's settlement, but was deemed too small, so the Pilgrims proceeded to the mainland and founded what became known as Plymouth, Massachusetts. Clark's Island today has a small number of homes on it, with some of the properties still in the family of the early settlers in 1620. The homes are self contained with no utilities and access is only by boat.

Several days later, we took a harbor cruise in Boston and learned about the fortification on Castle Island. There has been some type of fortification there since 1634. Edgar Allen Poe served here while he was in the Army. There was a local story of an officer being walled up in the dungeon after killing another officer in a duel. Poe allegedly used this story as the basis of his short story, *The Cask of Amontillado*.

I guess I need to find an island to write on soon, so I can finish this book.

Walking around the waterfront in Boston would not be complete without a pint of Guiness at The Black Rose, so we stopped there before meeting my daughter, Amber, and her boyfriend, John, for dinner and some Irish music.

Near the end of Base Camp, as I was explaining the schedule constraints that interrupted my three month walkabout, Rodg said, "Just look at it as all part of the walkabout. So what if you return home several times? You said you were going to be visiting family and friends and now some of the visits will happen at your home!"

That was a big lightbulb that showed me how my mind was erecting constraints for no good reason. So, my three month walkabout was immediately back on track. It no longer mattered that I would be retracing my steps. If I were wandering in the Australian Outback, I would inevitably be retracing my steps at some point. It turns out that retracing my steps was still a barrier to overcome.

On Thursday, September 1, 2011, Rodg and I packed our bags into my Smart car and headed west to Erie, PA. His journey would end the next day when he picked up his car in Erie and drove southwest to his home in Cincinnati, Ohio. My journey was just beginning in the town where I grew up and still enjoyed with family and friends.

The drive was uneventful, but it was good to have another driver along for the 560-mile journey.

Friends and family

Staying at Chris and Dave's as the first stop on my walkabout was a good decision. Chris and I are two of the 27 cousins on my Dad's side of the family. She and her husband, Dave, often provide me a place to stay when I visit Erie. My first night there I told them my plans and was just excited to voice my hopes and respond to their questions. It was great to feel their support and love. Chris asked the first tough question I heard on the walkabout.

"Do you mean you're actually trying to figure out what you want to do with your life?" I said, "Absolutely; for almost forty years the structure of my life has been built around my children and my marriage. That has now changed and I have to figure out what I want to think about first in the morning. Because Kitty is gone and Cooper is in his college routine, I'll always be there for the kids anytime they need me but it's no longer going to be on a daily basis.

So what do I want to do next? I still have unfinished goals with my Second Hope project about facing serious illness."

Chris asked, "And what about your Christmas trees?"

"That's also part of it. It takes several days work about three times a year to take care of the trees. And I know I can also fill up my time with volunteering but I don't see that as very challenging. When I had lunch with my friend, Wendy, who just lost her husband six months ago, I told her I know I can survive but I want to thrive. Just like I did all my life before Kitty died."

Chris then considered the possibility of what she would do facing a similar situation. She works in a church office and loves what she does, working for a pastor who is an excellent role model of what a Christian minister should be. So, for her, it was hard to imagine being faced with doing something different. Which is a pretty good position to be in, no matter how you look at it.

Friday, September 2, 2011

I went to the cemetery in the afternoon. I talked aloud at my parents' graves and told them about my walkabout. I asked them for their help and guidance. I also thanked them for all the wonderful love and constant support they gave me for so many years.

I went to my wife Kitty's grave and told her about my walkabout. I thanked her for putting up with all my crazy dreams and schemes over the years. I told her I wanted to be a better person now than I have been since she died and make more of an impact on all the problems we are facing today. I told her that

I had witnessed and done everything I could do for the first three items on her bucket list.

1. Amber graduated from college and started her professional life.

2. Remlee and Steve are married and enjoying their lives together. Watching them is a complete joy to me. They are like you and I were together during all our lives.

3. Cooper graduated from high school with high honors and is off to Villanova University and thriving.

4. I'm sorry I can't be a witness to the fourth thing you had on your bucket list, which was to grow old with me. I feel such profound and everlasting loss without you, Kitty. But I know I can't be stuck in that and I have to move on and create my own bucket list. I know I will see you again in heaven and we both want that to be a long, long, long, long time from now. This was my promise to Kitty about a month before she died, when she accepted that she might not be able to beat her cancer. She made me promise not to follow her for a long, long, long, long time so I could be there for our children as long as possible. A promise I intend to keep.

As I stood there at her gravesite, high upon a hill, with a distant view of Lake Erie, I also told Kitty that my future might include a relationship with another woman. I do not see how I could find another relationship as good as the one we had together. But I'm not going to worry about that or try to make a comparison or compromise.

I know I must open my mind and heart to a new partnership. I have not done that yet, despite some efforts at relationships. So, in my walkabout, I need to figure out (after lots of other priorities) what my criteria are for a committed relationship.

I finished the day off back at Chris and Dave's house, along with Chris' Mom, my Aunt Char. You would never know that Aunt Char is in her mid-80s. All her energy and enthusiasm continue to make her one of the most fun, interesting people to hang out with. She is the last of the generation before me, so any time I get to spend with her is treasured. Growing up, she and her husband, Ted, were the best example of how to have fun with your kids while still developing character, integrity, and family values. Just being around them and my other aunts and uncles provided so many different positive role models in my life. For the second time in my life, I played the card game euchre with Chris, Dave, and Aunt Char, which is big among all my cousins. I'm not sure why I never picked it up, since my Dad loved the game also. Apparently, it's an easy game to learn, as Aunt Char and I won. Or, maybe I was just lucky, as Chris pointed out.

Saturday, September 3, 2011

I picked up my friend, Cindy, at her house and we were headed to George's restaurant. I met Cindy several years ago at a wedding. When I told her I had known the family ever since high school and had baby-sat the bride and her sister, she said she had introduced the bride and groom. She said it was the seventh couple that she had introduced who had subsequently got married! She had previously mentioned that she was divorced and I said, "Wow! That's quite a matchmaking record. Why not look for someone for yourself?"

She said, "Nope, I'm done. Do you want me to find someone for you?"

I immediately said, "No, no thanks, not even thinking about that yet." But, over the next few years, Cindy and I became very good friends and she continued to encourage me to start dating. Eventually, I told her she was my best new friend this millennium.

But, back to this day. When she said she wanted Belgian waffles, I said that's a long shot at George's. She suggested Perkins and I agreed. As soon as we sat down, cousin Chris walked over to our table! She and Dave and Dave's family were seated on the other side of the glass partition. After we ordered, I went over to meet Dave's family.

Other than this chance meeting being coincidental, it was also fortuitous, as I had left their house that morning without my cell phone and a few other things I needed for my day. So, they gave me the key code to enter through the garage door. Funny how looking for Belgian Waffles can solve other problems you have!

Cindy challenged me several times today about how I would know what was true or valid as I was looking for a committed relationship. How would I know if I was dealing with someone truly committed to wanting a relationship rather than a financial advantage? Who could capture me?

At first, I explained that I had very little experience with women and could be too inexperienced to judge. But then, I thought of the outcome, not the initial screening process. That's when I was able to say that I was a pro at relationships. I had a great one for almost

40 years. So, while I would not compare any one woman to Kitty, I was a pro at having a great relationship and could not be easily misled.

Cindy asked what I would do if I found someone who is attractive in every way, physically, spiritually, emotionally, and totally into me. I said I was unsure but that the description was incomplete for me. Those are all wonderful characteristics, but I did not want someone who was just into me. A partner would have to have her own passions and interests outside of me. She should also understand and accept my need for people and places and things that did not match hers. I told Cindy I would send her a cell phone picture that explained the relationship. The picture could explain our own relationship as well as a living-together relationship. The picture is of two Ferraris. Two luxury, expensive cars - each with their own power and color. Significant and attractive in their own selves, but side-by-side, a bigger force than either would be on their own.

When I took Cindy home, I drove past Grandpa and Grandma Crowe's house at 1140 E. 30th St. I told Cindy a few stories of the 27 cousins and seeing the inside of the house in 2009. During our Crowe cousin's reunion in July 2009, several carloads of the cousins went on a tour of the family houses. Jerry and Lou's on Pennsylvania Ave., my parents, Dick and Thel's 719 Rosedale, Ray and Kay's on E. 38th St., Charlotte and Ted's 3950 Rice Ave. and Grandpa and Grandma's.

So, in 2009, as we were standing on the sidewalk by our grandparents' house, a minivan drove into the driveway. A woman and several teenagers got out and we went over and introduced ourselves.

The current owner is an African-American woman who runs a foster home there. My brother, Rodg, has her name and has since corresponded with her. Much of the woodwork in the house is the same. The most striking thing is the kitchen table with benches along the wall on two sides. The bench seats lift up for storage underneath. We all remembered sitting on those benches as kids! At any point on a Saturday or Sunday, there could be 8-10 kids jammed around that little table. We walked around the house remembering stories that happened there in the 1950s and 1960s, well over half a century ago. I remember picking bright red currants there in the garden and hauling stones for Grandpa to build an outdoor barbecue. It seemed fitting that a house that provided shelter, comfort and fun for 27 grandchildren was now being used in a similar manner by yet another generation.

After I dropped Cindy off, I did a few errands and went to visit another friend, Mary. Mary and I drove to Presque Isle Peninsula on Lake Erie and took a 3 1/2 mile walk on the bike path. We took a little ride around the Peninsula and went to the Marina where my friends, Bruce and Kate, keep their sailboat. I should get better about calling them in advance, as they have always invited me to go out on the boat with them.

Mary and I then went to the Cove Restaurant at the Sheraton Hotel on the other side of the Bay. Such a great view! Good food and reasonable prices by Boston standards. Near the end of the meal, I spotted sailing masts and we could see two tall ships. One was the replica of the "Niagara", famous as Admiral Perry's flagship in the War of 1812 and Mary said the smaller one was the "Pride of Baltimore."

We walked around the dock area and talked about the good features of it and the not so good. Mary thought the key to making it all better was the GAF property west of the convention center. It had been used for decades to manufacture housing shingles. The GAF Corporation had stopped using it several years ago and a local government body is trying to clean up the site and find a developer for the 12-acre property.

I wanted to tell Mary what I thought should be put on the property. For many years, I have challenged my mind to look at issues, problems and opportunities and imagine what it would take to resolve them. Sort of the "If I Were a Rich Man" game that many of us play from time to time. For this property, I had imagined an entertainment complex that captured the excitement of so many of the local Erie hotspots for dining, dancing, and amusement that made growing up there such a rich experience, even though most of us never had any money. The complex could be dominated by a destination attraction that would attract visitors from a wider region. But I refrained. Doing something like that would be contingent on having a lot of money, which can only come my way by winning the lottery. So rather than appear to be a pipe dreamer, I remained silent as always.

My conversations with Mary were a great invigorating way to explore the issues of what lies ahead and the different ways to find it. She is now divorced and coming off the end of a two to three-year relationship. My friends Wendy, Cindy, Mary, Becky and I all face common issues of being alone, having adult children we want to support, and deciding how to spend our time. The answers do not come easily or quickly, but I feel very blessed to have these wonderful women to talk to and feel supported and try to support them. Our past has not prepared us to become some undefined "significant other" in opposite sex relationships. Both Wendy and Mary talked about developing circles of friends of women who are either divorced or widowed. But I feel a far more powerful circle of friends would include both men and women. Our history and culture could prevent this, but there's no reason it is not possible.

Right now, I feel far more supported by my women friends than I do by my male friends. Why is this? I have always tried to resist the cultural stereotyping of women as more nurturing, supportive, and better at dealing with emotions rather than facts. But, the past few years and the new friendships I have developed with women seem to support those general notions. So, I wonder how that plays into my future.

Sunday, September 4, 2011

Joe was one of my best friends growing up. One of the events in Erie was a wedding for Joe and Kathi's daughter, Nicky. I sat at a table with a dozen long-time friends. All of the men in the group had gone to high school with Nicky's Dad, Joe. I had known Joe since about second grade, and miss him still. All of us were thinking of Joe and how much he would have loved to be there to walk his daughter down the aisle. But, Joe lost his battle with prostate cancer in 2002, after a courageous five year campaign. Joe was the best dancer of all of us, so we all felt his presence on the dance floor.

I am sure he got the biggest kick out of watching me in a ten minute blur that someone had to explain to me later. I was standing at the bar waiting for a drink when I heard my name being called over the loud speaker system. Several friends waved for me to go to the dance floor. It was empty except for Scot, the groom. I had not met him yet, so I walked up and introduced myself. He said, so you knew Joe from high school? I said even longer. We grew up about five houses apart, so I had known him since I was about eight years old. I started to tell Scot a story about our old neighborhood, but he was looking over my shoulder. I turned and saw two young men standing there; one was the stepson of Joe's brother, George.

It was then that I noticed the garter in Scot's hand and realized I was supposed to be with the other two single guys there to catch the garter! I walked back to them and they said, "OK, rock, paper, scissors." Not wanting to be seen as totally clueless, I started the game, "One, two, three." My scissors cut their paper. "Great, what did I win?" "You lose. You have to catch the garter!" I shook my head and turned back to look at Scot. One of the guys tapped my shoulder and pointed behind me. The garter was on the ground behind me! No drum roll, nothing. So, I picked it up and held it aloft as all my friends laughed.

I was walking back to my table trying to figure out what I was going to do with a garter. I wasn't seeing it hang from my rear view mirror. Duh! Someone grabbed me and steered me back to the dance floor, where a beautiful young girl was sitting on a chair. Ah, she caught the bouquet and was waiting to have the garter put on her leg. I winced as I remembered this ritual and the accompanying cheers to push it as high as possible, something about every inch above the knee was five good years of marriage. I knew there was good reason for me never to have put myself in this position before!

I introduced myself and said, "OK, how high can I put this?" She said, "How about just above the ankle?" Just then, Kathi appeared and gave me her sternest mock look and said, "This is my niece, Marty, you be nice to her." I laughed and held the garter in the air, which actually provoked a drum roll. Then, I got down on one knee and quickly slipped the garter about five inches above her knee! I stood up and gave her a hug and kissed Kathi.

As I walked back to my table, hoping my public embarrassment was over, Linda D. and Linda K. each grabbed one of my arms and turned me back to the dance floor where *The Electric Slide* was just beginning. Another first time fiasco to get through! I managed to mimic my way as well as several other novices did, although I don't remember the name of the woman I kicked. Probably best to leave it at that.

Monday, September 5, 2011

Labor Day was a day off for most people, but it was one of the days I had planned to do some work at my Christmas Tree Farm. I had purchased ten acres of land just south of Erie in February 2006. In May of 2006, about 15 of my friends and family helped me plant 2000 Christmas trees there. I had done this to keep myself connected to the city where I grew up. I also figured the 2000 trees would help offset the carbon footprint that my family placed on the earth. During 2007, I had made 11 trips to Erie to see my Mother during her last year of life. On each of those trips, I had stopped at the tree farm to do some mowing, pruning, and shaping of trees. After my Mom died in November, 2007, at the age of 96, my visits to Erie settled back to the more normal 3-4 times a year.

Although I tried to do some work at the tree farm on each of these visits, quite often weather would intervene and I would not be able to do much. This time, it would be mechanical difficulties that would keep me from doing very much work. Because it had been awhile since my last visit, the battery in my brush hog mower had completely drained. So, all I was able to do was a little hand pruning, which was quite difficult due to the high grass that had grown up between the trees.

This was not the first time I had come to grips with the difficulties of being a farmer very distant from his fields. I had already concluded that I had learned about 25% of what I needed to know to be a farmer. The prospects of learning the other 75% were not particularly high!

Several years ago, I had reconnected with my high school girlfriend, Diana, through a convoluted series of coincidences. We had started dating, another venture that I found I was not very good at over a long distance. She had accompanied me to the wedding and gamely agreed to help at the tree farm. I thought I lost her in the tall grass several times as she foraged ahead, pruning as she waded through the tall grass.

In the evening, Diana and I met one of my high school friends, Jerry, and his wife, Linda, for dinner at one of my favorite chicken wing places. For some reason, you can find great wings at a dozen places in Erie, while on the South Shore of Boston, I had yet to find any decent wings. Jerry had known Diana in high school during the time we dated. If Diana could not find me or figure out what was going on with me, she would call Jerry, who always gave her a good answer. So, Jerry was kind of a big brother to her. Besides being the funniest person I ever knew, Jerry is a great story-teller. Facts were just a starting point, a guideline, if you will. So, he was a good wing man to have!

Jerry and Linda had been at the wedding the day before, but we wanted to get together one more time before I continued on my walkabout. In addition to dragging me through the Electric Slide, Linda had razzed me some about my hair, which was almost to my shoulders. As we departed outside the restaurant, Linda asked me if they were going to see me down in Florida in March or April. I said I wasn't sure about anything that far in the future. Jerry said, "Who knows, after your walkabout you may decide you belong back in the corporate world and take a full-time job again."

I said, "I could get a haircut, buy hard shoes, wear long pants. I could be somebody!"

As Jerry walked away, he said, "Yeah, I can see you now, sitting on a park bench, eating a box of chocolates!"

So, apparently my image still needs a bit of work.

Wednesday, September 7, 2011

As I drove along Interstate 90 heading east back to my home in Kingston, MA, I reflected on all the conversations I had with people who had known me for a long time. Explaining my walkabout and my search for purpose came naturally with all of them, but how would it sound to a complete stranger? Would I even disclose it to a complete stranger?

I had wanted to spend time in Erie to sort out what role the city might have in my future. It had played a significant role in my life until 1970, when my wife and I left it so that I could take a teaching job in Illinois. We had continued to return every year and spend time with family and friends. Even though we had lived in eight states since then, Erie still felt like home. The cost of living there is quite a bit less than south of Boston and I know more people there than anywhere else. What would it be like living there again in retirement? Would I be able to make that decision?

As I passed an exit marked for Cooperstown, New York, my mind drifted back to a visit to the Baseball Hall of Fame. My mind goes back like it was yesterday. I am twelve years old and we are on our way back from camping for two weeks at Lafayette Campground in Franconia Notch, New Hampshire. It was a great trip: my parents and us five kids. We went hiking and swimming every day and ate around the camp fire where my mother cooked everything on a grill or in a dutch oven. One of the last nights in camp, rain was forecasted, so my brother, Rodg, and I dug a little trench around the tent to divert the water. It had actually worked very well and we stayed high and dry on our cots we borrowed from the Boy Scouts.

Packing up this morning was a little messy, as we had to take down and fold a very wet canvas tent and put all of our gear in the back of the Rambler station wagon. Dad surprised us all by saying we were making a stop at the Baseball Hall of Fame. Piling out of the car, we lined up at the door and got our marching orders. Mom would walk around with my two younger sisters and Dad would keep tabs on the older three.

Rodg, Kathy, and I set out to find everybody we had a baseball card for. Much to my chagrin, there were a lot of players here I had never heard of. But, seeing a few favorites like Dizzy Dean and Joe Dimaggio made it a lot of fun. Of course, we also knew Ty Cobb, Lou Gehrig and Babe Ruth, but no way could we afford one of their baseball cards. After a few hours, Mom is getting tired of amusing a nine-year old and a six-year old and I see Dad coming around a corner with that look that means we are leaving. So, I grab my brother's arm and pull him into an alcove. We put our backs to the main hall and start reading a display. Hey, I know this stuff!

I start reading it aloud, Rodg takes the second line and we take turns at every line;

Costello: I'm only asking you, who's the guy on first base?

Abbott: That's right.

Costello: OK.

Abbott: Alright. PAUSE

Costello: What's the guy's name on first base?

Abbott: No. What is on second.

Costello: I'm not asking you who's on second.

Abbott: Who's on first.

Costello: I don't know.

Abbott: He's on third, we're not talking about him.

We continued to the end of Abbott and Costello's classic routine, hearing laughter behind us all the time. As we finished reading, we had been laughing so much that our sides hurt. Turning around, there's my Dad, Mom, and three sisters and about twenty other people laughing and clapping for us!

Time to go! I'm standing on the sidewalk in front of the Museum. Mom herds us into a line and we all face Dad. "OK, kids, who's got money?" I say, "Who's on first." Dad starts laughing and says, "Empty your pockets. We may not have enough gas money to get home." I give up a dollar bill and some change. Rodg hands over a few bills and the girls all give what change or bills they have left in their pockets. The youngest, Karen, says, "All I have is a dime and a few pennies." Dad hesitated a moment and said, "That's just how much more we need."

We piled into the station wagon and headed west to Erie. It must have been enough because we made it home. I don't remember any of us kids getting a refund, but none of us would have asked for one. This was a time before credit cards or gasoline charge cards, so my parents had to estimate everything in advance for all our expenses. Stopping at the Baseball Hall of Fame was probably not in their budget, but they decided to do it because we had seen the sign on the way up and asked if we could stop.

As I continued on alone on my trip, I smiled at the memory of that day and the many times since that I had heard my Dad tell that story.

Trip to Florida

The next part of my walkabout was the one time that I knew I would not be able to focus solely on my own mission of facing my future. I would soon fly to Florida to see my sister, Kathy. I had not seen her since May of 2010, when I flew to Florida to be there during the last part of her son's three-year fight with cancer. Unfortunately, Scott passed away while I was waiting for my baggage at the Orlando airport. I arrived at Kathy's house just a few minutes before she and her other two children returned from the Hospice. The next few days of that trip were a flood of emotion that, for Kathy, still lasted over a year later.

For a long time, she was unable to even speak on the phone to anyone, and had been dealing with her pain and loss by avoiding any contact with people. Hopefully, my visit could help pull her a little bit forward.

As I arrived back home in Kingston, I received word that a cousin of my Dad had just passed away in Sebring, Florida, several hours away from Kathy's house. I had not seen Jeannine in several decades, but I remember her well from the first 18 years of my life. Jeannine had multiple sclerosis, which caused a few mobility problems for her, but she visited our family and my aunts and uncles many times, staying for months at a time. In hindsight, I think her visits were timed to new arrivals in the families and Jeannine came to help out. With 27 cousins on my Dad's side of the family, she visited often and we all got to know her very well. After the cousins stopped being born, Jeannine's visits tapered off. About that time, she began full time work at a Goodwill Industries store in Sebring, eventually rising to manager of the store.

My dilemma now was deciding to go to the funeral or not. I was pretty sure that Kathy would not be comfortable going, still enmeshed in her own grieving process. A portion of my walkabout that I thought was going to be a slight hiatus from thinking of my own purpose in life became a test of how my extended family fit into my purpose in life, not how it might distract me from my purpose.

I did not want to leave Kathy and her son, Brian, for a full day, but I have always felt strongly about representing my family at significant events like weddings and funerals. After many of my cousins, including myself, left Erie after our college days, weddings and funerals were the only places I saw some of them.

Still undecided, I packed for my flight to Florida. At the last minute, I put my suit back in the closet, telling myself I would still have other options if I decided to go to the funeral.

Thursday, September 8, 2011

The flight to Florida was uneventful, without any delays. As I sat putting my shoes back on after going through airport security, I watched another man collecting his things from the conveyer belt. He was a large African-American who looked like an NFL linebacker. He was wearing madras shorts sagging below his waistline. As he put each item, keys, phone, wallet, and so on into his pockets, the visible expanse of his boxer shorts grew to significant dimensions. Gravity was somehow being defied, but inexorably could not be denied. His activities were holding up the line and there were now at least five of us watching for the final drop. But, a security agent, who was also an African-American man, said, "Alright, Dude, get both hands on those shorts and pull them up, or I'll have you hauled off for indecent exposure."

They both laughed and the witnesses turned back to our own business as gravity was being interrupted.

As I drove from the Orlando airport, I reminded myself not to talk about my search for purpose very much, because I knew that Kathy's loss of her son was the dominant thing she was dealing with. Losing my wife was the most difficult thing I ever faced, but I still could not imagine losing a child. You can try to imagine, but you can never force your mind to focus on it long enough to get remotely close to how terrible it must be.

Kathy was one of my most steadfast supporters during my wife's illness and throughout my own grieving period through phone calls and letters. So, I was glad to finally be together with her to offer more than you can do by telephone, letters and emails. We talked late into the night and made it past that round of tears and fears.

Friday, September 9, 2011

My brother sent us the details of Jeannine's funeral service, which was scheduled for the next day. Later in the afternoon, I decided that I was going to go to the service. I asked Kathy if she wanted to go help me buy a few clothes so I wasn't wearing shorts and sneakers in church. I told her I understood that she might not want to go, which was fine with me. Later that night, she was still undecided as we told a few stories of how Jeannine watched over us, while our parents focused on our younger sister's births.

Saturday, September 10, 2011

At breakfast, Kathy told me she was going to go to the funeral with me, saying it would be hard on her, but she knew she needed to stop avoiding everything that was going on. On our ride to Sebring, she told me that she had driven Mom and Dad to see Jeannine several times in the 80s and 90s. Jeannine's service was a simple memorial Mass at her Catholic parish. Kathy and I spent some time after the service talking with a few of our cousins we remembered from our teenage years. Kathy was able to tell them about the loss of her son, albeit with a few tears. But, basically, she managed that process well. On the drive back to her home, she thanked me for bringing her along and said she was glad she came. Our cousins appreciated our coming to be there with them to celebrate Jeannine's life.

For me, the highlight of the trip was hearing several of my cousin's children speak at the Mass. I had never met any of this generation. They were in their late teens and early twenties, about the same age as Kathy and I were the last time we had seen Jeannine in our hometown of Erie. They told stories of their Aunt Neen, which is what we called her also. They talked about her taking them for ice cream and her insistence on managing her motorized wheel-chair herself, and racing ahead and making them run to catch up. They spoke about walking different places and talking about the birds and flowers on their way to the neighborhood ice cream stand. They talked about how Aunt Neen always asked about their schoolwork and what they were doing with their friends, and how much they laughed with her.

Every one of their stories sounded like one I could have told, but they did a better job of it because their experiences were still very fresh in their minds.

Sunday, September 11 to Wednesday September 14, 2011

Kathy, Brian and I left early to make a three and a half hour drive to the Jacksonville area. I wanted to see Kathy's other child while

I was in Florida. She had moved there several years ago, so my niece, Meghan, and her children, were not as easy to see when I visited Florida. We met at a park and had a picnic lunch in the shade. I could not help but think about the sharp contrast in all of their lives. Two years ago, there were ten of them that lived several miles apart, with Scott and Meghan's families side by side. Now, a year after Scott's death, Kathy and Brian were the only ones left in Sebastian, with the rest in Jacksonville, and Yellville, Arkansas. So, while losing her son was the worst thing Kathy had ever faced, the outward migration of her family intensified the problem, with little relief in sight.

I stayed another three days with Kathy and Brian. One day Kathy and I went to the Harbor Branch Institute in Ft. Pierce. Because of my interest in helping preserve ocean environments, I had received their newsletter for many years. I wanted to check out what kind of opportunities they had for volunteers. One idea I am exploring is to spend several months in Florida and do something to help the ocean. I knew that Harbor Branch had an ongoing project to rebuild coral reefs by growing live coral onto cement blocks that would then be placed in arrays in the ocean to create a new coral reef.

So, what part could I play in that project? I could learn to culture corals in the lab, attach them to the blocks, take water samples, move the blocks from the lab to a truck and then to a boat. Maybe I could even get my dive certificate renewed or just take the classes again. Why not? I still enjoy swimming and snorkeling. Learning some new scuba gear should not be that difficult. I picked up a volunteer form to complete and send in. My next stop was a dive shop where I got prices and a schedule for taking scuba diving lessons.

Kathy and I had many late night conversations after walking the ocean beaches during the day. Seeing the ocean waves roll in and out and watching the changing patterns of light as clouds rolled by has always been therapeutic for me. I saw a few small signs that it was doing the same thing for Kathy. Like meditation, if you just let these things come to you, it is possible to get outside of yourself and let a healing spirit enter.

Thursday, September 15, 2011

I had been thinking that I should make some effort to be a little more outgoing as I traveled, partially to bounce my walkabout experience off of people. And, partially, because I can go for days without talking to anybody. I routinely go through the self-checkout line at the grocery store so I don't have to talk to a clerk. I mean, how hard is it to exchange eight words with someone who is totally bored with their job? I had made a point of getting my sister out every day and into stores and situations where she would have to talk with people. As I drove to the Orlando airport for my flight back home, I thought, take your own medicine, brother!

Being stuck in a plane for several hours with someone shoulder to shoulder is an ideal place to engage in conversation. Fortunately, I fell asleep before the plane took off and I woke up when the plane touched down. So, I did not have to venture outside my comfort zone yet!

In a little less than a week, I had flown 2,800 miles and driven 1,100 miles, but it did not seem hectic to me. Somehow, I had found a rhythm within a maelstrom that invigorated me and left me ready for the next round.

2. Repack/Reload

Friday, September 16, 2011

After a late night load of laundry, it was easy to pack a small bag to go to Parent's Weekend at my son's college. My daughter, Remlee, and I headed out before noon to catch the flight to Philadelphia. We were both anxious to see Cooper in his new environment, with new friends, including a girlfriend for the first time! Of course, that's not counting the three or four girlfriends in junior high school. Cooper quickly figured out that those were meaningless because all you did was walk together between classes and eat lunch together. Both of which you could do without the label of "going out with..", or whatever his generation was calling it. His generation seemed to have this curious feature of a girl approaching a guy and telling him "Susie" wants to go out with you. If you accepted, you now had a girlfriend! So, was this a matchmaker or an agent? I could never figure it out.

Cooper had gone to an all male high school and only had several dates during that time. So, when he called me a week before this and said he had a girlfriend, I said, "Man, there are 4,000 girls on your campus! Take a look around before you latch on to someone." He assured me he knew what he was doing. Time will tell.

Remlee and I did meet the girlfriend, in theory anyway. There were two evening performances where she arrived early and saved seats for us. The logistics of seat proximity, not talking during the concerts, several assorted college friends being nearby, all of them engrossed in their I-Phones, apparently texting their friends who were not there, and all the college kids running off after the concerts resulted in one word (Hello) coming from the girlfriend. Neither Remlee nor I counted that as actually meeting the girl-friend – a sighting, possibly, but nothing more.

One of the concerts was a dueling pianos sing-along event, with lots of songs that I knew, but I'm not sure how many of the college students knew them. Afterwards, Cooper told me that the piano players were not very good. It took me a second to realize he was comparing them to his friend, Jeremy, who has won numerous piano competitions, including a performance scholarship to The Berklee School of Music in Boston. Cooper's grandmother on his mother's side is also a church organist, so most of his piano listening experiences have been either classical music or church music.

On Saturday, Cooper took us to a football game before we went to the evening performance, which was two of the improv actors/comedians from the TV show "Whose Line is it Anyway?" I was sure this was much more familiar to all the students than the honky tonk music from the night before.

Sunday, we did a little shopping at the King of Prussia Mall, apparently the second largest one in the country. I do very little shopping, so it is always interesting to have your children educate you about different stores, price points, and quality levels – none of which I need to know, but fun stuff, nonetheless. The afternoon soccer match was much more interesting!

It was great to spend some time with Cooper and see him fully enmeshed in this next stage of his life. He made it look very easy. I held no illusions that my next stage of life would be such a simple adjustment.

As Remlee and I flew home, we exchanged a few comparisons of our experience. It was clear that she had not yet adjusted to his absence in her life and his easy adaptation to living apart from his family. Her first few weeks of college were not easy for her, so I think she was relieved he did not have all the doubts and anxieties she had to work through when she was a freshman in college.

A Touch of Home

I decided to spend some time at home getting ready for the next phase of my walkabout. I wanted to do some camping along the way and I needed to get some more gear. I got recommendations from my daughters and their mates about mattresses, hiking shoes, etc. and did some online research before picking up what I needed at an Eastern Mountain Sports store.

Somehow, I managed to fill up five days with planning, shopping, making some plans to stay with friends along the way, paying some bills, getting tickets for a concert along the way, and who knows what else. Oh, I also met a few friends for walks or lunches.

I did spend a considerable amount of time looking through my road atlas, looking at possible routes to take. I did not want to spend a lot of time on Interstate highways. Many years ago, I had read *Blue Highways* by William Least Heat Moon. The book made an impression on me because of the types of things he saw and the experiences he had on the smaller highways. Ever since, I have often gone off the Interstate and taken local roads for a portion of my trips. You see a lot of America that is not visible from the highway system. My Dad very frequently preferred the state highways over the Interstates, particularly when there were tolls to pay!

I knew that my furthest destination to the northwest on this trip was going to be Detroit, Michigan. So, I pulled out my passport and decided to get there through Canada. I had five days on the road planned before my friends in Detroit were expecting me, so it seemed reasonable to head north to Montreal, then west to Toronto. I was going to camp along the way and just take my time seeing some new sights. In 2002, my wife, three kids and I had driven to Montreal as part of a well planned trip across the length of Canada by train. As we arrived in Canada, we discovered the Montreal Jazz Festival was going on! I know many people who plan for years to attend this event and here we just stumbled upon it on our way to a family wedding in Oregon. Our hotel was right in the middle of the venues. So, we walked around that evening taking in all the great music in the plazas and tumbling out of smaller venues.

Who knows what I might find through serendipity this time?

The night before I left, I thought about what I had experienced so far. I just let the activities and thought processes float around without trying to draw any conclusions. I had spent some very fun time with family and friends. I had helped my sister process some of her grief at losing her son at the age of 40. The trip to Jeannine's funeral was really a trip to the past and long ago family connections. I saw a glimpse of my son's future at Parent's Weekend.

So, what else lies ahead?

Saturday, September 24, 2011

It felt very strange not being with my son on his birthday for the first time ever, but that's part of the deal when your kids go off to college. Cutting the lawn myself was also apparently part of the deal. Between repacking the Smart car twice to fit in all my camping gear and then cutting the lawn, it was 2:30 PM before I finally got on the road. I headed west on Highway 44 before turning north on Route 140 to get to Route 2 West. My first stop was going to be Orange, MA. I was looking for a parachute jumping center that I had visited in 1977 when we moved to Massachusetts the first time.

Before we left Erie in 1970, I had taken jump lessons and had made three of the five required static line jumps that are required before you can pull the rip cord yourself. On the third jump, I came in hard and sprained my ankle. I was still on crutches when we left town to move to Illinois for a teaching job. I had looked at completing my training jumps in Illinois, but the price and distance were too much, similar to what I later discovered in Orange in 1977. So, this stop was purely nostalgic, not an attempt to complete unfinished business. As I drove, I remember bargaining with my son during the summer before when he expressed interest in skydiving. When I told him about my experience, he asked if I ever thought I would do it again. I hesitated and he asked if I would do it with him. For reasons I still do not understand, I said I would. I have not brought up the subject with him since. But, I have never gone back on my word with any of my children.

So, I picked up the 2011 brochures on the training program and doing tandem jumps with an instructor. Who knows what will happen? As I drove away, I remembered talking to an insurance salesman about life insurance many years ago, probably around 1972, when I was 26. After some preliminary questions, he started going through a list of health and activity questions. He came to a multipart question, "Have you ever scuba-dived, mountain-climbed, parachuted, or raced motorcycles?"

I said, "Yes."

He said, "Which one?"

"All of them."

"Oh, do you plan to do any of them in the future?"

"Probably, but I sold my motorcycle."

I don't remember the rest of the conversation or if that was actually the last question. But, I do know that I did not get that particular life insurance policy.

A month before I left on the walkabout, my son and I camped in Acadia National Park in Maine with my daughter. We have joined her boyfriend's family there for four or five years and there is a long mountain climb or bike ride every day. So, in about five weeks I have gone mountain climbing, gotten training information on scuba diving and parachute jumping. I'll keep my eyes out for motorcycle shops!

As I drove west on Massachusetts Route 2, I started getting an intermittent signal on my dashboard. It was the ABS warning light. I could not tell from the manual how serious this was, as it just said to take it to a dealer. I also encountered some road construction which slowed me down as darkness arrived. I stopped for the night at a hotel near Albany, NY.

The computer at the hotel revealed that there were multiple Smart car dealers in New York, Ohio and Michigan, but none were open on the next day, Sunday. I decided it would be better to stay in the U.S. rather than cross into Canada with fewer dealers. I also was not sure if my AAA Roadside coverage applied to Canada.

Sunday, September 25, 2011

I drove west on U.S. Route 20 through farm fields and apple orchards. Many of the orchards were teeming with people there to pick their own apples. I briefly thought about stopping, but figured I would probably be able to eat two apples before the rest spoiled in the heat of the car. I also saw an intriguing sign in front of a Mennonite Church – "All are Welcome". Knowing next to nothing about Mennonites other than a supposed similarity to the Amish, I thought a walkabout would be a good time to find out more about them. Unfortunately, it was about three hours after the service time, so I did not stop. But, what if I had stopped?

Although I was raised Catholic, I only occasionally go to church other than for weddings or funerals. But, I am openminded and have done some reading about many faiths and see the similarities at the core of their beliefs regarding ethics, values, and morals. The differences seem to be more at the periphery and the symbols used and the importance placed on key figures as deity or prophets.

I am fairly handy with carpentry and have done some stonework for walls and patios. I enjoy physical labor and have a wide range of cooking skills. I am already a tree farmer and willing to learn other agrarian skills. I don't watch much TV or drink coffee. I don't like talking on the telephone and much prefer conversation to radio or the Internet. I can abstain from alcohol for long periods of time. Since I enjoy camping, I don't need a fancy bed with thick mattress. I have helped take care of a horse and mucked out the stall. I know the difference between a pitchfork and a hayfork. Blue is my favorite color.

In fact, I'm probably a perfect candidate to become a Mennonite. Maybe I should look this up when I get back home to find out how many faiths I have irritated with my random musings. But, it keeps me awake on long drives!

Later in the day, I saw a sign for Hamilton, New York. Now, why did that sound familiar? It took about a mile for me to resurrect that from my 1960s memory storage bin. So, I did a U-turn which is very uncharacteristic of me. I rarely turn around and go back, but I was chastising myself for not turning around to see if there were any Mennonites still around the church. Rather than miss another opportunity, I turned the car around.

Hamilton, New York, is the home of Colgate University. I had visited here several times in 1964 and 1965. The details are lost to time or rather poorly entered into memory due to considerable partying there with Bob, my friend from high school, who had introduced me to my wife, and who was also Best Man at our wedding. But, the Stone Jug Bar is still there and still busy. The campus is still a beautiful place to walk around, but it is hillier than I remember. In those days, the drinking age in New York was 18, which was a great idea at the time, although not necessarily conducive to keeping scholarships intact.

As I drove back up the highway to Route 20, I was disappointed that I had not gone into the Stone Jug and had a beer and what I remembered as a very good cheeseburger. I tried to rationalize it as past lunch time, not yet dinner time, and I don't drink in the middle of the day. But, it troubled me that I was letting habits dictate certain aspects of my walkabout. Wasn't a walkabout the time to break out of your habits and try new things? Was I just going to travel around and look at things or was I actually going to do something new? Was I a spectator in life or a participant?

By this time, the sun was going down and I had to decide what I was going to do about getting the car repaired and, more importantly, where I was going to spend the night. I was in a part of the country where I have too many friends and family to consider paying for a hotel room. I had a cousin who had recently moved to Buffalo and offered his place as a way station on my trips to Erie. There was also a Smart car dealer in Buffalo that could repair the car. After considering the logistics of my cousin's location, the dealer's location, and walking into a car dealer repair shop without knowing more about the problem, I decided to delay the repair issue, since the warning light had only come on twice today.

A better choice seemed to be to drive a little further and see if I could stay at Diana's house in Mayville, NY. When I called, she said, "Did you call to congratulate me?"

I said, "Sure! What am I congratulating you for?"

"My Buffalo Bills just beat your New England Patriots!"

"Wow, I totally lost track of that game. How bad was it?"

"We were down by 21 points at one point, but we came back and intercepted Brady four times, including one for the go-ahead touchdown! Final score was 34 to 31."

"All right, then! Congratulations, I'm glad we didn't have a bet on that game."

"You got lucky this time. So, what are you calling for?"

"Would you like some company tonight? My travel plans changed."

I headed east on Route 20 to Mayville, NY. Within ten minutes, I drove right by the Buffalo Bills stadium. There were still several hundred people in the parking lot enjoying the second round of tailgate partying. I rolled down the window to listen to their whoops and cheers. Have fun, guys. We play you again this year.

I stayed in Mayville for three nights enjoying Diana's company and taking care of a few logistics. I called my mechanic back in Kingston and told him about my car problem. Walter at Monro Muffler does all my car work. After asking several questions, he assured me that the car was safe to drive, even though the ABS system was likely not functioning. As long as I had plenty of brake pedal and no hesitation in stopping, it would be fine. He also said I had to take it to a Smart car dealer, because general repair shops like his did not have access to the computer diagnostics necessary to isolate the problem.

With this information, I decided the repair could wait until I got to Cincinnati, where I would have access to my brother's car and not have to sit at a car dealer all day while the repair was done. I also got in touch with the new owner of the property next to my Christmas Tree farm in Erie. The prior owner let me store my brush hog in a shed on the property. I was glad the new owner granted me permission to continue using the shed, as I wasn't prepared to buy a shed and put it on my property. I did drive the forty miles into Erie to deal with the dead battery in my brush hog. I took the battery to the place where I bought the machine and wound up buying a new battery, but was left with little time to go back and do any work. So, the brush hog battery was added to the gear on my walkabout.

Instead of camping in Canada, I wound up in the relative luxury of a house on Lake Chautauqua, enjoying walks along the lake shore, playing tennis, going to a movie, and taking a ride on the Chautauqua Belle, a genuine paddle wheel boat that cruises the lake. This boat, like the one in Plymouth, Massachusetts, is one of only five in America that is propelled solely by the paddle wheels. All the rest have a different drive system and the paddle wheel rotates as a result of the boat moving forward.

Roughing it has never been quite this good!

3. RHYTHM OF THE ROAD

Wednesday, September 28, 2011

I left Mayville, NY heading northwest to Detroit. Driving past my hometown of Erie without stopping seemed totally weird. I had only done it once before, when Cooper and I were on a college tour going from Rochester to Pittsburgh. I was still interested in camping, so after passing Cleveland on Interstate 90, I got off onto Ohio Route 2, thinking I would spy a campground somewhere between Cleveland and Toledo. If there are any on that road, I missed them.

It was getting dark, so I decided to look for a motel. While driving near Sandusky, Ohio, I spotted a Motel 6 too late to get off the highway. Forge on or go back? I never turn around and go back. Oh, wait, what was I saying about old habits? I got off at the next exit and went back.

The motel had an Arby's right next door, so I picked up a sandwich and got to my hotel room in time to watch the season end badly for the Boston Red Sox. The Red Sox lost in the bottom of the ninth inning to Baltimore. The Red Sox were overtaken for the wild card spot by the Tampa Bay Rays, who were nine games behind them on September 1. The Red Sox lost 20 games in September, which must have set some kind of record. What an amazing meltdown! I had not watched any television since my walkabout began. I picked a bad day to pick up the remote!

Thursday, September 29, 2011

I continued driving west towards Toledo and stopped at Put-in-Bay to get some lunch and update my trip log. While sitting along Lake Erie, I decided I should come back to this spot and spend some time exploring the area. I was already behind schedule for my targeted arrival in Detroit. There are islands offshore and several airplane services that take off and land on the water, which is something I have never done.

My rough ideas of what I would be doing on my walkabout seemed largely to be wrong, but events were just creating a different path. Not altering my walkabout, but rather fulfilling it. I have to get over the idea of what should be happening on my walkabout, and embrace the idea of welcoming what is happening on the walkabout.

I noticed a time when driving today that I was not thinking of anything. Very rare, since I am generally either thinking of the past, negotiating the present, or imagining the future. When I realized this, I tried to go back to a state of thinking about nothing - and I did! That session lasted for another half hour. I realized this was very valuable and since then I've done it several more times. You create a vacuum and see what fills it. Once it was my Christmas tree farm, another time the Second Hope project, another time my kids. Finding what came out of the silence first seems a truer measure of importance than trying to grab some idea out of the constant rambling of an active mind.

When I got to West Bloomfield, Michigan, just north of Detroit to visit other old high school friends, Tom and Sandy, I relayed that incident to them. They both burst out laughing. I said okay what's so funny. Tom then explained that Sandy is always asking him what he's thinking about and he always or often says "nothing" and she doesn't believe him because her mind is always going on about something. So I reassured her that it is possible to think about nothing.

Many people use prayer or meditation or Eastern techniques like yoga, Zen, or tai chi, to empty the mind, body and spirit in order to relieve stress and be receptive to what is coming.

While my "nothing" episodes have not resulted in any great "aha's" arriving, I think it's part of the process and will continue to do it.

Talking with Tom and Sandy was energizing. Even Tom admitting that he was so focused on getting his health under control that he could not think of anything else like finding a purpose seemed to be insightful to him. We talked about what you would do differently in your life. Sandy thought she might get an accounting degree. Tom thought he might have been a lawyer focusing on corporate business issues and I thought of being a marine biologist.

Tom said he never thought of himself as a leader or that he was that outgoing as he grew up. But then he went into sales and became outgoing and a leader, rising to president of a manufacturing company. As for me, I was so afraid of speaking in public that I delayed taking a required speech class until my senior year of college. Several months later I became a schoolteacher and spoke in front of twenty kids every day! My entire professional career was as a teacher and a trainer in business and industry.

What does that tell you about our nature? Do we subconsciously move toward our fears even though we consciously try to distance ourselves from them? I am still sorting that one out.

But as we were talking about leadership, I asked Tom who was the leader of the pack in high school. He immediately said it was not him and we talked about how the group shifted around from ten or fifteen and higher sometimes. Tom said, "Maybe it was Jerry. He was always in the mix of things." I said, "Detz was certainly the funniest guy in the bunch and could lead us into some strange experiences. But, he was always spontaneous, not necessarily planning out our activities." Tom said, "What about Joe?"

"He's another possibility, but he and I rode together a lot, living around the corner from each other. It seems like we were both waiting on somebody else to come up with a plan."

We talked about a few other guys and big events we got into and could not come up with someone for the title of leader of the pack.

Tom and Sandy and I have known each other since high school. They are the type of friends whose lives may drift apart from mine without much contact for several years. But when you get back together, you easily pick up where you left off, as if you just saw them last week. So it was just great to hang out and enjoy each other's company. I did get there too late in the season to enjoy their swimming pool, which is where we hung out on previous visits. Tom thinks they bought the pool and were glad a house came with it. I was glad to feel at home with them wherever they have lived.

Find Inspiration

One day, we went into Detroit to take a tour of the Ford Motor River Rouge Plant. The tour starts with a bus ride from the Henry Ford Museum. Henry Ford built the plant in 1917. At that time, it was the largest integrated manufacturing complex in the world. It had more square feet under one roof than anywhere else in the world. It employed 100,000 people by the 1930s to build Model A cars. The plant was vertically integrated. Raw iron ore came in one end and finished cars came out the other end. Something like 95% of the parts used were manufactured on that site. It was a bold, innovative approach to manufacturing cars that served the Ford Motor Company well for over half a century.

As the automobile business evolved over the years, this approach became too cumbersome and ultimately cost prohibitive. Production began to shift to other factories that were built to assemble cars from parts built elsewhere by specialty facilities. By 2004, the world's largest manufacturing plant was no longer producing cars.

William Clay Ford Jr., the great-grandson of Henry Ford, decided to resurrect the River Rouge plant. Ford invested billions to rebuild the plant as a modern automated production facility that now produces 6000 Ford F150 trucks every day. The F150 has been the best selling truck in America since 1977. Since 1982, it has been the best selling vehicle in America, period!

As we walked above the assembly line on the tour, I was struck by the layout of each station. All the parts had to be available within a few feet of each operator, so that time was cut to a minimum. The storage bins had to be reloaded from a parallel path so that restocking would not interfere with the operator currently installing parts. Each station had a different number of actions to be taken, depending upon the amount of time each step took. This ensured that every station could complete the required tasks in the same amount of time because the assembly line never stopped moving.

It was also obvious that different types and colors of vehicles were interspersed along the assembly line. So, at the beginning of the body line and the door line, there had to be coordination, so that at the end, the right size and color of door had to match up with the right body. Decades of manufacturing experience and increasing automation, robotic machines and computer control has led to a highly successful operation where the amount of labor hours needed to produce a car continues to fall.

It seemed to me that the door assembly line had more stations than any other segment of the trucks. Who knew it took so many steps to put in the window assemblies, door locks, remote receiver, speakers, latches, handles?

My work as a trainer in business had involved developing considerable skill in analyzing jobs, breaking them down into sequential steps, and developing job aids, support materials, and training programs to support the jobs. But, in figurative comparison, I was dealing with twenty yards, not miles! It was hard to imagine the thousands of details that had to be analyzed to make this modern production line hum so efficiently.

Near the end of the tour, we stood in an observation deck that allows you a view of the entire complex. A tour guide pointed out a thick painted line in the parking lot. If you drive a Ford Motor Company product, you can park to the right of the line, closer to the employee entrance. If you drive a non-Ford vehicle, you have to park to the left of the painted line and have a longer walk to the employee entrance. The company cannot require all employees to drive a Ford product, but they don't have to make it easy for people who do not!

Saturday, October 1, 2011

Tom and Sandy were headed for the airport as I left to drive south to Cincinnati. They were flying to Myrtle Beach, South Carolina for an annual outing with a bunch of people from Erie. The outing has grown over the years to include seventy golfers, plus some nonplaying spouses. They take over several hotels and plan to play five rounds of golf during the week.

As they were organizing their luggage last night, they were measuring carry on bags and suitcases, trying to minimize the baggage fees. It finally amounted to just a little over the price each of them had already paid for their tickets. So, it was like taking a third person along. Fortunately, they only had to feed two of them, not the third baggage person!

As I headed south from Detroit, I thought of the section of Detroit that we drove through to get to the Henry Ford Museum where we caught a shuttle bus to the River Rouge plant tour. There was highway construction that forced us off our planned path. The GPS in Tom's car was only calibrated to physical roads, not socioeconomic conditions. So, we were on some residential streets that showed the scarring of the economic downturn that resulted in thousands of layoffs in the automobile industry. Many blocks had burned out buildings and empty lots where homes had been demolished. Boarded up windows and overgrown lawns showed other abandoned buildings, while broken porches revealed other houses that could no longer be entered.

Elderly people shuffled along the street pushing shopping carts with their few meager possessions. The blankness of their faces hid whatever emotions they were dealing with that day. The flotsam and jetsam of decaying urban life were visible everywhere for miles. The automobile industry was in turnaround mode, but I wondered what else had to happen to heal this urban decay and the wretchedness of life so many people were still stuck in. The order and precision of the manufacturing line I had just witnessed was a marvel of efficiency, but rebuilding a decaying urban area was not an assembly line process. But, could the lessons from the assembly line be applied in a different fashion to Detroit's socioeconomic problems?

As I pondered this paradox, I realized how helpless everyone is in the face of catastrophic change. How do individuals deal with it? How does the city government of Detroit deal with rising needs and declining revenue? What does Michigan do? What does the Federal Government do? Too many questions, too few answers.

Suddenly, I found myself on the Toledo Skyway Bridge over the Maumee River. It soars into the sky with three lanes of traffic on Interstate 280 in each direction and carries me to a new place. It leads me down a road new to me that will swiftly carry me to my next destination. It is an inspiring sight, an engineering marvel born out of a need and a vision executed by architects, engineers, builders, steelworkers, concrete workers, and highway builders. What does it take for Detroit's bridge to the future? Where does the visionary team come from and who will pay for it? More questions, no answers.

Several hours later, I passed an exit for the John Glenn Space Museum. I briefly thought of getting off at the next exit and going back. But, figuring how much time the museum would take me, I knew I would be driving in the dark to find my brother's place. So, I pressed on. Aach, old habits again. I need to get better at looking ahead, or leaving more space for the unexpected to be embraced.

Driving down Interstate 75 near Monroe, Ohio, I was surprised to see a damaged metal frame or tower off the side of the highway. When I saw a church behind it, it suddenly dawned on me that this is where we saw the huge statue of Jesus when we traveled this road in 2005. When I reached my brother's apartment, I asked him about it. He said it was called "Touchdown Jesus" because the arms were raised skyward, but it got struck by lightning last year and destroyed by fire.

Wow, can you imagine that? What does that mean? Rodg said it was pretty controversial among the church members, but they decided to rebuild it. It must have sparked a few discussions about God's feelings about the wisdom of a 70-foot statue advertising their church. How do we sort out these signals in life, from God, or otherwise? In this case, you could make an argument for persistence in the face of adversity and rebuild. Or, you could make an argument to accept the change and move on. I wonder how often

I have made choices that I only recognized later as a turning point. Most times, the turning points are not marked by the drama of a lightning bolt, are they? But, very often, the turning points require acceptance or perseverance. Which is the right path?

Being with Rodg another four days at his apartment in Cincinnati was again uplifting. We seem to rotate between meaningful topics, a few current events, and periods of silence. All with equal comfort and benefits. It was good to see his daughter Christy and her husband, Brendon, in their new house (a mansion, actually). His son, Dave, joined us for the day, as well.

They have a small garden plot on which everyone in the family has been sharing the work, learning together about organic techniques and sharing work. It is a good thing that connects them all together, including Rodg's ex-wife, Judy, and her new husband, Lloyd. They have a blended family situation that works well for everyone. At one point, Judy talked about getting "grounded," more connected to the earth because of the garden. She even took her shoes off in the driveway and I said, "But now you have to dance around in circles." Of course, as Remlee pointed out later, I should have suggested she might get better results if she actually stood on the grass! Asphalt might actually be an impediment to grounding.

After lunch, I talked to everyone about my Second Hope book about facing serious illness. It is based on our family's experiences during my wife's illness. I had received feedback from several reviewers that it was actually a love story and perhaps should be shaped in that direction. Brendon said it sounds like a movie! I realized later I should have asked right then if he wanted to produce it. He and his business partners have actually produced six or seven movies for TV family-friendly fare. But I talked more about the elements of the book and people offered ideas about it. Brendon's production process is market research driven since their biggest sponsors are a consumer products manufacturer and a large retailer. I knew this and thought if I talked more about the visual elements of Second Hope that Brendon might get more intrigued. But he did not and the moment passed.

As I'm writing this portion, I am thinking about how I am missing things, not connecting the dots, not being aggressive enough, not asking for what I want. It's a long-standing barrier, this reluctance to engage. It hurt my consulting business and has kept me from aggressively pursuing a book publisher or agent for the Second Hope manuscript. Is this fear of rejection the next thing I have to overcome? What else keeps me from achieving any of the other purposes I seem to want?

On a lighter note, Rodg took me one day to Lunken Field, which used to be the main Cincinnati airport. They have some exhibits showcasing the development of aviation, as well as the difficulties of building an airfield in the triangle of where two rivers meet. Today, the airport serves the general aviation industry and houses corporate aircraft for large companies like Procter & Gamble.

A sign in the lobby offers the opportunity to join the mile-high club. For a mere $450, you and a partner can be whisked a mile high and a discreet pilot watches the horizon while you and your partner celebrate your bodies in whatever fashion you choose.

Harkening back to a simpler time, my brother and I took a scenic ride along the Ohio River on U.S. Route 52. Our first stop was at the birthplace of Ulysses S. Grant at Point Pleasant, Ohio. The simple house is still standing and the small town remains much the same as when Grant was born. It was a little hard to compare the historic General and President to these humble surroundings that were far from any centers of population, commerce, or influence. But that can be said for quite a few of our presidents, including two of the last three.

Somewhere between Utopia (really!) and Higginsport, we took a ferryboat across the river at Boudes Ferry, which began service about 1798. It was a short ride across the Ohio River to Augusta, Kentucky. Just as in the 1800s, the ferry crosses the river whenever traffic shows up and needs to cross. We were the third car that showed up and a few more joined us, plus two trucks, by the time the ferry arrived in about five minutes. The crossing only took about ten minutes. The $5 fee saved us about 45 minutes driving to the next bridge and backtracking to Augusta. Augusta has a quaint historic downtown area with period houses, restaurants, and shopping. It also has the homestead of Rosemary Clooney, preserved as a museum, including artifacts from when her nephew, George Clooney stayed with her. If I were a bigger George Clooney fan, I would have paid the admission fee. In hindsight, I should have paid it because I have seen more films of Rosemary Clooney than George Clooney. Maybe next time.

As we returned by ferry to the Ohio shore, I realized that we could follow Route 52 and several other highways along the river all the way to Pittsburgh. If an 18th century boat left Pittsburgh averaging five miles an hour heading west on the Ohio River and a car heads east from Utopia averaging 42 miles an hour, at what mile marker can the car driver throw an apple to the boat captain, assuming the river length from Pittsburgh to Utopia is 370 miles?

On the way back to Cincinnati, we stopped at the Captain Anthony Meldahl Lock and Dam between Chilo and Neville. We were hoping to see one of the long strings of barges traverse the locks, but all we sighted was one cabin cruiser heading upstream. In the 1800s, most of the boats on the river were heading downstream, opening up the western frontier. After their cargo was offloaded at their final destination, the boats were dismantled and the wood was used to build homes or barns.

It makes you wonder about the mentality of the captain and crew on these early cargo vessels. Do you plan on becoming a settler once you get there? Or do you look for passengers hoping to settle or travel further westward? Or, do you buy a horse when you get there and ride back, through unknown territory? How much food and water do you start out with? Do you follow the river back? If so, you are traveling three miles an hour and need to stop every twelve hours, say. At what mile marker can you hope the captain of a boat leaving Pittsburgh at the same time will toss you an apple?

In this context, my choices seem relatively simple, but how do you put it all into a word problem? So, no matter what technologies exist at any given point in time, there are always risks and unknown factors to deal with as you move forward in life.

Another way of looking at choices is to pull out your key ring. How many keys do you have and what are they for? Monday night, I was sitting at the bar of a British beer pub, having something to eat and a few beers with my brother, Rodg, and his son, Dave. Dave used to manage an Irish pub and gave me a short description of what a "perfect pint" of Guinness entails. The beer has to be drifted down the side of the glass in stages, so that the head does not get too big.

The pour has to be stopped at the exact right time and the pint is allowed to settle while the foam achieves a crown rising above the rim of the glass without spilling over. This often requires the patience of the beer drinker who may be watching his pint get perfect for several minutes.

The beers in front of us looked just about perfect to me, but Dave cautioned me to give it an extra minute. While I was waiting, I pulled out my key ring and said, "Another way of looking at my walkabout is to determine what I would do if I lost my key ring. What would I fight to get back? Keys tell a lot about the responsibilities you have in life. Do they hold you back or propel you forward?"

I put my key ring on the bar and Dave said, "That's it? You have one key and a bottle opener?"

"Yep, that's my house key."

"But… no car key?"

"The car is at the dealership getting repaired, and if I never saw it again, it would not matter."

"So, what does the little bottle opener tell you about your responsibilities?" Dave asked.

I replied, "I have a responsibility to be healthy enough to be there to support my kids and have a beer occasionally!"

Dave pulled out his key ring and said, "Whoa, I have too many responsibilities!" He started describing each key, many of them work-related and found several he never used anymore and one that he was not sure what it went to. He said he would have to look them over and see which ones he could do without, because it was a pain sorting through them to find the right key sometimes.

Having too many keys can easily be a distraction from what is important in our lives. For me, my key ring has become a symbol for what I want to focus on. There are several keys that I only need several times a year, so why carry them every day? For example, the key for my brush hog sits in a small gear bag that I take with me when I go to the tree farm. Perhaps the next step to clearing out unnecessary things that distract me from my purpose in life is to clean out my garage. Now, that is truly a scary thought, as I know there are several boxes out there with inventory tags from three or four movers. And, the boxes have not been opened any time between tags!

The Vacuum

Wednesday, October 5, 2011

I had spent too much time on the Interstate highways getting here, so I left Cincinnati and headed back east on Ohio Route 32. The view is mostly farmland, interspersed by a few small towns along the way. As you approach Athens, Ohio, the road becomes U.S. Route 50. I had been to Athens several times in 1966. My wife, Kitty, started her freshman year of college there in September that year. She was not planning on going to college, but I had gotten cold feet in July that year and had backed off getting married in August. While I drove to California, looking for the truth about my feelings, her parents got her enrolled at Ohio University in Athens.

She was not at all happy to be there, still struggling with the abrupt shift from planning our wedding to living away from home as a college student.

I returned to Erie and her in August, but another plan had been set in place. We wrote each other constantly and talked on the phone occasionally. When I visited her in October, we both decided we should get married as soon as possible and make our lives together. So, I returned a week later and brought her back to Erie. In hindsight, it was all rather adolescent and a more moderate approach would have been for her to at least finish the first semester and get the credits. But, it all worked out, despite our parents' great dismay at our actions.

As I approached the town of Athens, I debated about stopping there for the night. But after driving around campus and only seeing a few familiar sites, I decided not to stay there. Visiting old familiar places is always good, but neither Kitty nor I had any happy memories of her time there, so I continued east towards West Virginia. I was still looking for my first camping spot on the walkabout. My map showed a state park with camping near Cairo, West Virginia, not too far from the border with Ohio.

As I drove south on West Virginia 31, the road got narrower and narrower. The houses got smaller and more run down. The town of Cairo has one gas station and maybe four businesses that are still open. The rest of the small downtown area was boarded up or looked abandoned. I had not stocked my little cooler with anything to cook for dinner that night, but most state park campgrounds have a small store with hot dogs and a few other essentials.

As I continued out of Cairo, the road up to the North Bend State Park got even narrower. Houses at the side of the road could only be reached by driving across a shallow creek. My doubts about camping there continued to increase. At the top of the rise, I suddenly came upon a parking lot with about 40 cars in it. Much to my surprise, there was a lodge there with a restaurant and a full parking lot. I checked a map board and headed toward the campground. There was no activity at the campground at all, which had apparently closed for the season. I decided not to check out the housing situation at the lodge and to continue looking for a campsite. As I returned to the park entrance, I got a phone call from my son. Knowing that I could not drive down the narrow entrance road and talk on the phone, I pulled to the side of the parking lot. I would have lost cell phone coverage as soon as I got off the hill anyway.

I was due to pick Cooper up two days later for his fall break from college, so he was checking on the timing of that. Most of our phone calls are short and oriented to logistics, but we both wanted to catch up on what was going on, as it had been several weeks without any contact. After about 15 minutes, I reluctantly said goodbye as I realized I only had about an hour to get down the hillside and find another campground.

The hour came and went and I did not see any signs along Route 50 for a campground. As I approached Clarksburg, West Virginia, I gave up the camping idea and headed north on Interstate 79 in the growing darkness. The easy driving on the Interstate quickly brought me to Morgantown and I turned east again on Interstate 68. I was looking for a Days Inn or a Red Roof Inn, both of which have predictable prices and quality. But, I was also reflecting on the day's drive and my reaction to the rural mountains of West Virginia, so I may have missed seeing one of them.

About ninety minutes later, I wound up stopping at a Red Roof Inn in Cumberland, Maryland. It was around 9 PM by this time, so I decided to get a sandwich somewhere to eat in my hotel room. When I returned to the hotel with my sandwich, I stopped in the parking lot and looked up at a cloudless sky. As I gazed across the sky, wishing I knew more constellations than the Big Dipper and Perseus, a shooting star blazed across the sky. It was the brightest, longest view I ever had of a meteorite entering our atmosphere.

So, I was at a good place to be that night. I thought of all the times I could have stopped this day and thanked my lucky stars I had not!

I also wondered why I had still not unfolded my tent. Camping was an essential part of my walkabout plan, but I had not done it in the first five weeks. I know there were myriad decision points that brought me to this spot. What is the difference between executing a plan for your life and just going with the flow of life? I was not so concerned about this question in the context of my walkabout. I was concerned about this question as I faced my future. Just going with the flow is always easier, but you never know where you could wind up. My mind balked at examining the question any further and I floated off to sleep with the image of the best shooting star ever still bright in my soul.

Thursday, October 6, 2011

I was not due at my friend's house in Berkeley Springs, West Virginia, until the evening, so I decided to take a steam train ride. This historic steam train ride goes west from Cumberland to Frostburg. As it rises in the hills, you get a panoramic view of the valley and you see why this area was a key part of the westward migration.

The Visitor Center in downtown Cumberland has a museum that showcases the historic role the city played in the westward migration. George Washington and Thomas Jefferson both talked about a roadway into the interior of the country. Thomas Jefferson signed the act that established the National Road. The road was the first federally funded road in our history and was designed to connect Cumberland, Maryland to the Ohio Valley. It was built between 1811 and 1834.

The second major pathway through Cumberland was the arrival of the Baltimore and Ohio Railroad in 1842. It was followed in 1850 by the opening of the Chesapeake and Ohio Canal. The canal brought settlers and goods from the Washington, DC area by mule drawn canal boats, which hauled farm goods back to Washington. The original plan included extending the canal all the way to Pittsburgh, but the engineering and expense required to do that kept that part from ever being done. The success of the National Road, most of which is now part of U.S. 40 all the way across America, and the westward expansion of the railroad, eventually spelled the demise of the canal.

According to the National Park Service website, the seven day trip from Cumberland to Georgetown was a long and demanding journey. Most of the family's eighteen-hour day was devoted to moving the cargo, mostly coal, down the canal. Because the boat was designed for cargo, those aboard had to content themselves with the smallest of accommodations: a 12'x12' cabin was the family's quarters for the trip. Although small, the cabin contained all the necessities: a coal burning stove, bunk beds with hay mattresses, a table, and a small cupboard for supplies. The boats also included a stable for the mules and a hay storage area.

To reach Cumberland, canal engineers began near the nation's capital in 1828 to construct 184.5 miles of ditch and towpath. They built 74 locks, 7 dams, 11 aqueducts and a 3,118-foot tunnel--remarkable achievements with the tools of the day. As each dam was completed, diverting water from the Potomac River into the canal, boats began using the watered sections.

With the canal open and the railroad flourishing, both of which fed traffic to the National Road, Cumberland developed many support industries including boat building and repair, as well as manufacturing related to the railroad industry.

The steam railroad now operating as a tourist attraction is run by the Western Maryland Railway Company. The train travels to Frostburg, Maryland, where it is turned around on a turntable for the return trip down the mountain. You can take your bicycle onboard and ride back to Cumberland, or you can continue riding on the Chesapeake and Ohio Canal Bikepath. The bike path follows the original towpath of the canal for much of the way and goes from Washington, D.C. to Cumberland, MD over 180 miles.

There is an hour and a half layover at the terminal in Frostburg, which is enough time to grab a bite to eat, do some gift shopping, and tour the small museum which houses the horse drawn carriages used during the 19th century. Within a very short span of time and distance, you can see all the technological changes which happened to bring our lives from a three mile per hour pace to today's sixty five mile an hour lifestyle. The technology changes in transportation have left many of the small towns along the path of the canal and railroad in much the same state as they were in the boom period of 1880 to 1920, with the boom long since over.

As we descended the mountain back to Cumberland, I stood in an open freight car and leaned out a doorway window. I imagined traveling this way, or perhaps on a canal boat, trying to imagine what life was like back in those days. Does a slower and simpler pace reduce life to a less stressful level enough to balance the tradeoff in time? The wind shifted and I was engulfed in smoke from the engine. The tradeoff equation was not looking so good at this point!

But, I could not help but compare my situation to the changes that many of these towns along the canal faced. Because the canal traffic faded away, the core purposes of the towns were no longer viable. Because my daily caretaking role was over, a major purpose in my life was no longer needed. The towns had to shift their focus in order to remain viable, but their location was fixed as well as specific skill sets. What new skills did I need to learn to be viable? And, was my location also fixed in place?

After a short walk along the canal, I spent time in the visitor's center absorbing the pictures and stories of a time gone by. In another 100 years, will there be museums full of quaint stories and pictures of our obsolete 550-mile an hour airplanes and a primitive communication system based on the Internet, with long-forgotten companies like Yahoo, Google, Microsoft, Dell, and Facebook?

It was a short drive from Cumberland, Maryland to Berkeley Springs, West Virginia. My friend, Jill, lives on a farm south of

Berkeley Springs. I have known Jill since 1975, when I hired her to perform at a Cultural Barn Raising at West Virginia State College, where I was a faculty member. We have remained good friends, although many years can roll by without getting together. I had stopped to see her in July on my way back from North Carolina.

When she greeted me this time, she gave me a long hug and said, "The problem with living by yourself is not enough hugs." I replied by squeezing her harder and saying, "Boy, ain't that the truth we face every day."

It was good to be with Jill Thursday night and Friday morning. We had another great conversation, just like the last one in July. Both of us feel a greater purpose in life is ahead of us. I realized Jill was preparing for hers by eating healthy, staying physically fit, meditating and staying positive. She talks of putting positive energy out and, in return, good things will happen. It struck me that my walkabout was a similar process and I had specific purposes that I was investigating whereas hers were general. On the flip side, she was still actively engaged in her art of performance and artistic creation, while I was again searching for that daily avocation.

Nonetheless, both process and outcomes have a similar impact – positive energy that can inspire more people to put out positive energy.

So, is there a life force that is shared that is driving many people forward (or has us spinning our wheels in one place)? Perhaps Jung's collective unconsciousness is it. I'll have to research this further. Maybe all my imagined barriers are physical and mental constraints and there's another path through the unconscious that I could take. I am thinking now of my life dream that has driven so many of my actions in the past. It seems too overwhelming to layer that into my thoughts now. But perhaps the key is in there.

As I think of all the ideas and expectations that Jill and I shared over the course of about eight hours of conversation, I wondered how many other people there are that wrestle with these same inquiries into the purpose of our lives. And how seldom even good friends engage in these explorations. Why don't we do it more often? Why don't we do it with more people? More realistically, why don't I do it more often? I have taken many opportunities over the last month to do it and have now become comfortable with the process. Can I sustain it as part of my lifelong learning process?

Both Jill and I are open to what is coming next for each of us. The answer may be unclear, but we are both preparing ourselves for it.

Friday, October 7, 2011

I set out in the morning for the four-hour drive to Philadelphia to pick up my son for his fall break from college. I got off Interstate 81 near Chambersburg to head east on the Lincoln Highway, U.S. Route 30. I decided not to stop at the Gettysburg National Military Park since I had been there several years ago. Just after I passed York, Pennsylvania, I was surprised to see a house built in the shape of a shoe! Was this the old lady who lived in a shoe? No, it was an advertising gimmick of Mahlon Haines, who had built a regional chain of shoe stores. I had seen this building in a book or a video of unusual buildings several years ago, but had forgotten where it was – Hallam, Pennsylvania.

Our drives between Philadelphia and home seemed to vary from seven to ten hours depending upon time of day, traffic conditions, and weather. I was hoping for a trip closer to the low number. Unfortunately, due to his class schedule, we could not beat the rush hour traffic out of town and wound up with an eight-hour trip. But, I also had his undivided attention during the ride (aside from his two hour nap). Undivided is actually a relative term when you are talking about a 19 year old with an iPhone. Nonetheless, we did get to trade stories about what we had been doing and what decisions were uppermost in our minds. Listening to Cooper talk about his courses and his thoughts about his college major brought back lots of memories of my own college and career choices. And here I was doing a similar search myself for a new life direction. I'm not sure if that is just ironic or is it also apropos?

What am I going to major in next?

Checkpoint

After a late night arrival home on Friday, Saturday was just a day to unpack the car, get laundry started and attend to the minutiae of life like sorting the mail and paying bills, but more importantly figuring out when to see my daughters. Although it was good to be home, leaving some things in the car, like the camping gear, also gave me the excitement of knowing I would head back on the walkabout in one week. But before I could attend to the future, I had to spend some solid time in the present and reconnect with all three children and a few friends. And, also look at the recent past and see what I had experienced so far on my walkabout. I knew that I had a great time, but did I learn anything that would help shape my purpose in life?

I have been puzzled in recent years why the logistics of returning from a vacation now can take several days. When I was working full time, we always returned from vacation on Sunday evening, unpacked everything and went back to work on Monday. But now, when I don't have to go back to work, it takes two days to unpack the car and duffel bags, do the laundry, process the mail, pay bills, and get new groceries. Granted, my wife and I did all these tasks jointly in prior years. But, I don't remember it being any big deal. Perhaps I am just less efficient on my own. It can't be because I am slowing down!

One part of getting back into a routine was to read the newspapers that had accumulated. Remlee had been getting the mail and newspapers while I was gone. I should be able to toss most of the newspapers because most of the news had caught up to me at some point. When I travel, I always buy local newspapers because I am used to reading at least one every day. But, I paid for my hometown newspaper and had to read it. After about ten of them I realized I was reading headlines on each page and very few stories, plus I was skipping the sports pages entirely. I decided that when I returned to the walkabout the following week, I was going to put the paper delivery on hold. If I was building a different life, I needed to look at all of my habits, many of which are not productive.

I made plans to see several friends for lunch or dinner. I looked forward to telling them about my walkabout. But I realized when I was talking to them that some of the certainties I had experienced now sounded vague and incomplete. My friends seemed to be looking for conclusions or statements of purpose or new goals to go after. I had none of that to offer yet, even when they asked if there was one thing I had settled on. After parting, I pondered whether I was withholding information from them or had I not really learned anything yet? This bothered me because these friends are women I have shared a lot with and have no reason to conceal things from.

It took me several days of periodically reviewing my conversations before it struck me. They were looking for news about the end result and I was not even thinking about the end result yet. I was still figuring out the process and had not tried to formulate any purposes or new goals. I was still picking up driftwood with no idea of how to assemble the pieces into a raft that could float, or better yet, a sailing ship.

My conversations with my three children were much more comfortable. They seemed glad I had a focal point for what I wanted to do. The fact that I was happy and engaged in a process was more satisfying to them than whether or not I had reached any conclusions.

The Process

So, what had I learned about the process? I had stepped outside of my normal environment and left a daily routine. I had turned off all my gadgets. I did not take a laptop. I carried a cell phone, but it was turned off much of the time. I asked friends and family not to call me. My three children were the only ones I told to call whenever they wanted to. I was never going to limit their access to me.

I had visited family and friends and talked with them about what I was hoping to find. I celebrated a new marriage in a family I care deeply about. Many of my best friends joined in that celebration. I also joined with a long disconnected family to celebrate the life of a person I knew well when I was younger. I helped my sister process grief of an unknowably intense nature.

I learned to listen to the rhythm of the road by not listening to music, news, or anything at all as I was driving. Like most people, I am not used to nothing going on. We all have a different affinity for different levels of activity around us. I found a way to embrace nothing and wait to see what pops up in my head. Silence can be golden. Out of the silence, my mind could wander without the pressing confines of what I should be doing next. There are always lists of things to be done somewhere. I left those lists behind.

I looked for things to inspire me, like the Ford River Rouge plant, the islands of Lake Erie, and the Toledo Skyway Bridge across the Maumee River, and historical places like President Grant's birth-place. Both River Rouge and the Skyway Bridge seemed to be the impossible made real. I was merely looking for something that seemed very possible to me, yet I felt like I was standing on the shoreline without any tools in hand. It was time to look at the tools I did have.

I recorded my thoughts in a variety of ways. I kept a journal. I kept a trip logbook with the details of where I stayed, how much money I spent and how much exercise I got. I also recorded thoughts and sightings by an audio recorder and shaky notes in my calendar book. As I drove, if I was frustrated by not gaining any new insights, I reminded myself that this was just practice. I had to practice, practice, practice before I got good at confronting my future. It was valuable to create a vacuum and see what got sucked in. I was looking for the old ideas that would not go away, but excited to see what new ideas would emerge.

As I began to pack for the next stage of my walkabout, I reminded myself to be patient and let the process work. It was necessary to:

1. Step outside of my normal routine.
2. Turn off the gadgets.
3. Listen to the rhythm of the road.
4. Embrace silence to create a vacuum.
5. Let the mind wander.
6. Seek inspiration.
7. Welcome new ideas.
8. Record to remember.

4. Head for Water

I finished up a few final details, like signing and sending the papers to the insurance company so we did not have to pay car insurance on Cooper when he had no access to a car back at college. I also reserved a room for our traditional two days of skiing at Peek n' Peak near Erie after Christmas.

I repacked my duffel bag and added it to the camping gear still in the car. I decided after dropping Cooper in Philadelphia that I would head east to the Atlantic Ocean and follow the coastline as closely as possible all the way to Florida. The ocean is like a magnet to me; many of my most inspiring, joyful life experiences have been accompanied by the sound of ocean waves.

Sunday, October 16, 2011

Cooper had pretty much lived out of his duffel bag for the week, so it was easy for him to toss what he had worn in the washer and dryer and put them back in the bag. Although he had enjoyed his week visiting his friends and sisters, it was easy to tell he was excited to be returning to his friends (and girlfriend) and get back into his college routine where he was thriving.

The drive back to Philadelphia was only about six and a half hours, one of the shortest trips so far. After a quick meal at Qdoba, a Mexican restaurant, I dropped Cooper off at his dorm room and headed east to Atlantic City, New Jersey. Why not start this leg of the walkabout with a little gambling? If I hit it big, I could fund some of the wilder schemes on my list of ideas that do not go away. Besides, the room at the Trump Marino Casino was only $48 including tax, about half the price of hotel rooms in Philadelphia.

When I arrived at the Casino, I discovered it was being converted to a Golden Nugget Casino and there was construction going on in the lobby and elsewhere. I am not sure if that explains the low price or if the New Jersey casinos are luring gamblers with low room rates.

After I took my bag to my room, I wandered around the casino looking for the one-armed bandit that had my name on it. I always look for one with only three rotating symbols, including cherries, bars, or bells. It also has to have a pull arm. Old school. There is nothing more boring than pushing a button to make the wheels spin.

I look at playing slot machines as an entertainment; I am willing to pay twenty dollars per night to be amused. Some nights arc shorter than others, but this night had my twenty dollars bounce up and down four or five times over several hours. Boredom finally set in and I cashed out with seventeen dollars. When you cash out, it makes the sound of quarters falling into a tray, but it just prints you a ticket to redeem at a machine or teller. A cheap fling with a hint of nostalgia.

Monday, October 17, 2011

I drove around Atlantic City and stopped to take a four-mile walk up and down the Boardwalk. Through the misting rain, I saw that most of the businesses were closed for the season. It was hard to envision throngs of happy tourists shuffling between cotton candy, fried dough and hot dogs. I did hear a few plaintive wails of children wanting something out of reach of their parents' interests. I also realized that with the exception of the casinos along the boardwalk, all the rest were geographically separate from one another. In fact, they seem to be concrete islands with no means of access other than by private car or tour bus. Casinos apparently want you to come and be captured, with no easy means of leaving for another casino. It is well known that there are no windows or clocks in casinos, so that patrons have no reminders of the passage of time. The physical barriers between competing casinos are another way to wall us off from the real world.

This may be good for business, but it definitely detracts from the experience of exploring multiple places to have fun. Driving and walking around, it was fun to see all the streets from the game of Monopoly. Well, almost all of them. I saw Baltic and Mediterranean, Indiana and the Carolinas, but somehow missed Park Place, the biggest real estate catch of them all. I hope that's not an omen!

The mist turned into a light drizzle and I decided it was time to head south. I had no target for the day, as my only plan was to go to my sister's house in Florida and hug the coastline all the way. Route 619 goes down the barrier island which is commonly called the Jersey Shore. It goes through Ocean City, Sea Isle City, Avalon, and Wildwood on its way to Cape May. As I drove through these communities, I was struck by how well maintained all the properties are. Although most of the properties were built back in the fifties and sixties, they look freshly painted in vibrant colors, with well-maintained small lawns or flower gardens in front. Many of them are rental properties for the summer season and perhaps competition keeps property owners vigilant about maintenance. It was like driving through a movie set!

I turned onto the Garden State Parkway for the last few miles to the ferry terminal at Cape May. Several miles before I got to Cape May, I noticed in the periphery of my vision a large bird taking flight from the median of the roadway. I immediately knew it was a Great Blue Heron. I also knew I was on a collision course to hit it. I immediately jammed on the brakes and swerved to my right into the breakdown lane. In that slow motion that can happen in emergency situations, I saw the beating of his wings, the single eye facing me, and a wingspan that exceeded the width of my Smart car. The Great Blue Heron rose slightly and swerved to my left as I swerved right and it glided just a few feet above me.

In my panic, I had slowed to 40 miles an hour and never rose above 45 miles an hour during my last few miles into the Cape May ferry parking lot. I had been several feet from killing a Great Blue Heron, a bird I had grown to love from our days of living on Melbourne Beach in Florida. Given my feelings for the ocean and the environment, I am thankful for my periphery vision, my reaction speed and my physical ability to respond to danger. Without these, I would be doomed to reconciling my path in life with the death of a majestic bird that has inspired me and everyone in my family.

We had all grown very fond of Great Blue Herons after seeing them almost every day when we lived on the beach in Melbourne Beach, Florida. My own safety did not occur to me until a month later when I told this story to my daughter, Remlee. She quickly pointed out that the bird could have smashed the windshield and done some harm to me as well. Yet another reason to be vigilant.

The ferry terminal at Cape May is one of the best on the east coast. As you drive in, everything is very well marked so there is no confusion about what lane to go in or where to get tickets. The terminal itself is a modern structure with high ceilings and tall windows that allow you to see the panoramic view of Delaware Bay and all the activity that takes place there. It is large enough with many outside seating areas, so you do not feel pressed among the hundreds of people waiting for the next ferry.

Whenever I take a ferry, I always relax after leaving the dock. Here, I was able to relax during the wait and simply enjoy the view of the water. As we proceeded across Delaware Bay, I noticed a long line of ocean freighters simply sitting in the water. They were waiting their turn to go up the Delaware River to the shipping docks in Wilmington, Delaware and further upstream in Philadelphia. It made me wonder who the traffic cop was that controlled this shipping lane? It would require cooperation between the states of New Jersey, Delaware, and Pennsylvania, multiple port authorities and dozens of private enterprises involved in loading, unloading, warehousing, fueling and servicing. Add in U.S. Customs and Homeland Security and the Coast Guard and you quickly have increasing layers of complexity.

It makes you wonder how importing foreign goods is economically feasible. Somebody has to pay for all this. Which is us, of course, either through buying imported goods or paying our taxes. There's a lesson here somewhere that I need to think about more.

The ferry ride is actually considered part of U.S. Route 9. After debarking from the ferry, I followed Route 9 for a short distance and then turned south on Delaware Route 1. I had no target destination for the evening, so I continued along the shoreline, stopping every so often to get a better view of the ocean at Sussex Shores and Fenwick Island.

As I crossed into Maryland, the ocean road changed to Maryland Route 528 with the same great views of the ocean occasionally. At Ocean City, I headed west on U.S. Route 50 for a short distance before turning south on U.S. Route 113. The view dramatically changed as I headed away from the ocean into the interior of the Delmarva Peninsula. Farmland and a few woods now dominated the landscape. This view was broken up occasionally by going through small towns like Ironshire, Snow Hill, and Beaver Dam. Driving through towns like these, I try to figure out how they survive. Sometimes, you can see factories, lumber mills, or a large office complex that helps explain why people are able to live there. But, quite often, it is a mystery as to what incomes exist to support the grocery store, hardware store, two restaurants, and five bars in town. And, there are usually at least three churches to choose from in all these small towns.

Shortly before crossing into Virginia, I merged onto U.S. Route 13. Although the Delmarva Peninsula narrows considerably at this point, you are still distant from the ocean and do not catch any glimpses of it until close to the Chesapeake Bay Bridge and Tunnel. It was on the late side of dusk and I decided to find another motel, rather than try to find a campground and pitch the tent in the dark.

I did not act quickly enough on selecting a hotel and found myself on the approach to the bridge. As I began my trip across the bridge, I realized the problem I had created. Crossing the Chesapeake Bay by bridge and tunnel is an awe-inspiring trip. Here, again, the impossible was made real by a group of people who saw the value of bridging this twenty-mile opening of Chesapeake Bay into the Atlantic Ocean. A team of visionaries, architects, and engineers worked with the political entities to develop a vision and a plan to connect these landmasses without disrupting an already busy shipping channel.

It took twelve years, but the bridge opened to vehicular traffic in 1964. Originally one lane in each direction, a parallel bridge was built and opened in 1999 to accommodate two lanes in each direction. I had crossed the bridge several times in the past in daylight. Crossing it at night was not as awe-inspiring, even though you do get this sense of being alone on the ocean in the dark of your car.

I found a hotel room for the same $48 price as the Trump Casino. There was no construction going on at the Best Value Inn in Norfolk, but it was quite a bit less sumptuous and had no slot machines. A Mexican restaurant next door offered reasonable prices. I briefly debated eating there, but the television was blaring, so I decided to take my meal back to the hotel room. I had avoided watching any television on the walkabout so far (except for the last 15 minutes of the Boston Red Sox season) and saw no reason to start with some forgettable sitcom.

Tuesday, October 18, 2011

As I ate my Mexican meal in my room last night, I decided to fix my error of the night before. Once again, I would do the unthinkable and backtrack on the same highway. It was twelve miles back to the Chesapeake Bay Bridge and I paid the toll again. The day was sunny and bright and I drove to the rest stop about half way across. The fishing pier was full of people casting their lines into the water. I saw more people catching other people's lines than actual fish, but as my Uncle Ted often said, "It was a good time to catch fish." He would say that about high tide, low tide, rainy day, cloudy day, or sunny day. It was all about the experience, not the result. At his funeral, his youngest son, Terry, was telling the story of fishing with his Dad for small mouth bass on the Bay in Erie. Terry cast his line out multiple times right where his Dad said to. But, he was several feet off the mark his Dad indicated. So, his Dad cast his line right on the mark. Zing, whirr, in comes the fish!

I said, "Terry, I lived that story myself. In fact, there are probably five of our cousins who had the exact same experience as your great story. Your Dad taught us all to fly fish at that same spot off the pumping station!"

In April, come trout season, if your line wasn't in the water at the 5:00 AM opening of the season, you were not a true fisherman, according to Uncle Ted. Then, he would catch his limit for the day while some of us were waiting for our first bite. Between him, my Dad, and Uncle Ray (Ted's brother), the fishing stories became family legend. Do you remember when Ray...? Always a good time!

As I walked around and read the signs telling about how and when the whole bridge and tunnel system was built, I saw about ten freighters offshore who seemed to be waiting their turn to go in and unload. So here the harbormaster had all the same complexity as the one in the Delaware Bay, with the added layer of complications of a major U.S. Navy Base. Several years ago, I watched in awe as an aircraft carrier went through the channel. Newport News, Virginia is the busiest naval port in the world. In addition, there are shipbuilding and maintenance facilities, as well as multiple dry docks. I am sure there are many times every year when commercial shipping interests are delayed due to national security needs.

I was now satisfied that my backtracking up the highway was well worth the time. Seeing one of the world's most magnificent man-made structures is something not to be missed when the opportunity presents itself. Turning south again, I found Route 168, which took me into North Carolina. In Barco, the road merges into U.S. Route 158. There are several spots where the road is close enough for a view of Currituck Sound, which is between the mainland and the Outer Banks of North Carolina.

At Point Harbor, the road turns directly east across a causeway to the Outer Banks just above Kitty Hawk. I stopped at the Visitor's bureau and heard a state trooper tell someone that the beach road was open now. There was a temporary bridge at one point, but all the damage to the roads from Hurricane Irene in August had been repaired.

I headed north on Route 12 through Duck and Sanderling, looking for the area where we had stayed in 1999. My wife and I organized a family reunion to pull her family together in the waning days of her father's life. Tony had congestive heart failure and it was uncertain how much longer he had. His nieces and their families from Long Island came, as well as his daughter and two grandchildren from Ecuador. My wife and our three children came down from Massachusetts. All fifteen of us shared two rented houses, played different games and went to the beach every day. Mostly, we enjoyed each other's company.

One day, many of us went on a party fishing boat out of Oregon Inlet. We came back with a huge mess of fish for a fish fry. It was the only time in my life when I cleaned and filleted more than eighty fish at one time!

We had rented a wheel chair with big balloon tires so that Tony could join us on the beach. Kitty's Mom, Dorothy, was upset when it looked like the dune buggy chair would not fit through the bridge walkway to the beach. One of the niece's husbands, Mike, is a pretty big guy, and between us, we lifted the chair with Tony in it, high enough to clear the obstruction. When we arrived at our lounging spot near the ocean, I pulled the flag off the dune buggy chair and planted it in the sand. I then proclaimed this land as far as the eye can see to be known hereafter as Tony Onisko Beach.

We had already named the reunion as the Double O, to commemorate the Oniskos at the Outer Banks. Adding a named beach to the historic occasion seemed the proper thing to do. Sadly, Tony passed away about a month after the reunion. But, he was filled with warm family memories just before the end.

I saw many familiar sights as I drove around Duck and Sanderling and Corolla, but I did not find the houses we had rented and there was no sign up for Tony Onisko Beach. But, I did find all the memories.

I also found a Travelodge in Kill Devil Hills, just a stone's throw from the ocean. I paid for two nights because the third day was predicted to be rainy, windy, and cold. For most of the walkabout, I have been eating from the deli counter of grocery stores, plus a few takeout places. Now that I was at the ocean side, I decided to sample a few of the local places for seafood. The first night, I found a brewpub with an excellent fish special as well as several very good craft beers. I had been eating lightly and exercising every day. But my second night in Kitty Hawk was a departure from the norm.

Jimmy's Seafood Buffet was bustling, even though it was well past tourist season. The buffet was loaded with every type of seafood imaginable and I sampled every one of them. Some of them three times! When I got back to the hotel, I decided to take a beach walk to work off some of the thousands of calories I had just consumed. For some reason, I kept sinking deep into the sand, which made walking difficult. Probably some effect of the tides! I went back up to the roadway to walk on a firmer surface. I would have to increase my walking miles for several more days to break even, but it was well worth it.

The next day, I ate a late lunch at the Nags Head Pier and called it the meal of the day. I had decided to stay a third night in Kitty Hawk, even though the weather forecast was the same. I would have to drive pretty far to find anything better. So, I took a drive down Beach Road 12 to see some of the area that took the heaviest damage from Hurricane Irene.

When I went downstairs that evening to use a computer, there were two women with long white canes standing by the elevator. They were talking and laughing up a storm. I said hello and asked if they were going downstairs. I pressed the elevator button and as they heard me move, one of them said, "I told you it was on the left, not the right!" The other one said, "You also said that about our room and our room is on the right!"

The first one said, "We figured someone would come along sooner or later and rescue us!" They continued laughing and joking on the ride to the lobby. When the door opened in the lobby, someone said, "There you are! We were about to send out the St. Bernards." Looking around, I saw another dozen people with long white canes. Another twenty were outside getting into a charter bus.

The computer in the lobby was available and I sat down to check the weather and send an e-mail to my kids. I could hear Cash Cab on the TV behind me and I only missed one of about 30 questions. I think I should have stopped in New York City on the way down and looked for a cab! I talked to Scott, the night manager of the hotel. He said the large group that was here was a visually impaired group that comes every year. They fill up five hotels and have two charter buses and they have a great time. It is a mix of people who are completely blind, legally blind, or visually impaired in some way. There is a large contingent of volunteers with normal sight who accompany them and assist where needed. He said he looks forward to their coming every year, because they all have so much fun together.

I thought that volunteering for such an outing could be fulfilling, as well as challenging. Many of the historical or inspiring places I had visited on the walkabout immediately educated me, primarily because of what I could see. For all of these visually challenged people, they needed to absorb information from sounds and touch.

There are also a few people still staying here after Hurricane Irene flooded their homes in August. The flooded homes were more on the sound side than on the ocean side. One woman just checked out at 7 PM because her house was finally ready after two months of repairs and paperwork.

I asked Scott about the temporary bridge south of Oregon Inlet. He said there were actually four new inlets that were broken through the barrier island by Hurricane Irene. Two were closed up right away with sand and bulldozers and a new roadway was laid down. The temporary bridge spanned the other two new inlets and will be there about five years before a permanent bridge is built. I think they want to see what the shifting sands and waters do during that time before they come up with the new bridge design. I also read that Hurricane Irene actually deepened part of Oregon Inlet from six to eight feet, thus saving money on planned dredging.

I told Scott about an area in Rodanthe (pronounced with a long "e" at the end). It was on the west side of the highway in an area that had lost its access road and driveways. He said right across the street from there was the house used in the movie "Nights in Rodanthe." The house had been moved further south and west from its original location due to damage from Hurricane Earl last year. It is still oceanfront property and the owner is asking a premium for people to stay in the house that was used in the movie. I never saw the movie, but will have to check it out.

When I returned to my room, I took out the last dollar bill in my money clip and added it to a pile of change for the hotel housekeeper. I left in the morning without a penny in my pocket. It reminded me of my boyhood trip from the Baseball Hall of Fame in Cooperstown heading back home. But, I had something in my pocket that my parents did not. Thank goodness for ATM cards!

Friday, October 21, 2011

I again headed south on Beach Route 12, heading towards Cape Hatteras. Once again, I had no target destination in mind. I had seen the Cape Hatteras Lighthouse several times over the years, but had not seen it since it was moved back from the sea in 1999.

Due to storm erosion and predicted rising sea levels, the lighthouse was jacked up on heavy timbers and moved back from the sea to preserve it for future generations. Due to recent heavy rains, half the parking lot and an area right next to the lighthouse were flooded. Standing next to the lighthouse, you cannot see the ocean; so, much of the beauty, grandeur and history seemed to be lost. The light can still be seen from the ocean and still serves as a landmark and warning to oceangoing ships.

I continued driving south to the free ferry from Hatteras to Ocracoke Island. It is a short 45-minute ride across the gap. The North Carolina Ferry system is a reliable service of a combination of free and toll ferries that connect the mainland and all the various pieces of the Outer Banks. At this time of year, all cars and passengers are accommodated, but during the summer, reservations are a better bet. There is nothing worse than missing a ferry and looking for accommodations in high tourist season.

Well, there are lots of worse things, but for a traveler in a hurry, it is pretty bad.

Ocracoke Island is not too big and it only takes about 25 minutes to drive down it to the next ferry. I stopped at a small viewing area overlooking a pen where some wild horses were grazing in the grass. The horses are a part of the herds that stretch along the coastal islands, including Chincoteague in Virginia, famous from Marguerite Henry's book *Misty of Chincoteague*. The horses are the descendents of horses the Spaniards brought over in the 1500s. Each year, some of the horses are rounded up by driving them into the Sound and corralling them on the other side. They are then sold at auction to the highest bidder. This is done to control the size of the herd. It is also an event that attracts upwards of 40,000 tourists.

Looking at these wild horses penned up so that tourists could see them left me puzzled. What's wrong with this picture? Wild horses do not belong in a pen, do they?

The ferry from Ocracoke to Cedar Island on the mainland takes about two and a quarter hours. Being on the ocean is always a pleasure for me, so the time factor of ferries is never important. There is always a new view to explore as I walk around the boat. I am always mystified on car ferries at the people who sit in their cars the entire time, trying to talk on a cell phone that inevitably goes out of range of the cell towers. They are not allowed to have the engines running, so it must get hot inside the car. I recently read about a newly defined group of people who get fast food and then eat in their car. I forget what marketers were now calling this group, but they are trying to understand this group, in order to better market products to them. The marketers should take these long car ferries. They would have a captive audience of people who love staying in their cars!

As we pulled off the ferry at Cedar Island, I stopped to go inside the terminal. There was a small gift shop there where we had purchased some glasses many years ago. Mine were still in service, but I thought they would be great gifts for several of my friends. The glasses have images of all the North Carolina lighthouses on them, and are perfect for a good rum punch. Unfortunately, the terminal was already closed so I continued down Route 12 until I reached Route 70. Although I was still close to the ocean in an area with the same climate as the Outer Banks, the look of the land had changed. Not the land itself, but the types of buildings and the uses of the land. All the homes were smaller; year round residences, and the marine-related businesses were for small boats and local fishermen, not expensive yachts or cruisers. There were very few restaurants or motels and no tourist gift shops. Everything had changed from tourist to working class.

It was not too long before the surroundings shifted again. As the road approaches Beaufort, North Carolina, the emphasis on tourism returns, although most of the beachside houses do not approach the size of many on the Outer Banks. As darkness approached, I pulled into a motel at Atlantic Beach that promised a clean room and a TV. Good enough for one night. Even better, the room had a small refrigerator and sink and a table, which was perfect for a dinner of cheese and fruit from my cooler.

After my simple meal, I sat at the table and played a long session of the game If I Were a Rich Man. I do this periodically to stretch my thinking of what things are possible. It even works sometimes on small problems when I realize that there are better solutions to some issues than spending money. In this case, I was using it to explore some ideas that would not go away and force myself to examine if they could play a role in my future.

If I Were a Rich Man

The first thing I would do is form a management company for a core group of four to six people that I have worked with over the years, to guide the development plans for all the projects to be undertaken. I already have a list of twenty-four projects that I have thought about over the years. Next, I would form two non-profit organizations to do the work of Second Hope Wellness and Community Opportunity Conferences. Second Hope Wellness would publish my book on facing serious illness. The Second Hope Approach to Facing Serious Illness is based on our experiences during my wife's illness in 2004 and 2005.

The Second Hope Approach is the system that can build strength in people to either cure them, or make them strong enough to give the first hope (medical care and your own immune system) more time to be successful. This book describes an approach to systematically pulling together all the resources needed from multiple places to deal with all aspects of a serious illness. Second Hope is an organized approach to meeting the needs for organization and record keeping, education about the illness, physical fitness (diet and exercise), a family and friends support system, the power of laughter, visualizations for wellness, and spiritual power.

I have already written and produced The Second Hope Guidebook, which is a binder system to keep all relevant documents and notes about a serious illness in one binder that can be carried to all medical appointments.

Second Hope Wellness would develop a plan for two major projects, a home within a hospital for the families of people facing serious illness. Family could stay there nearby their loved ones. It could be next to care units or completely integrated with care, which I am leaning towards. The second project is the Longest Roads Second Hope Tour. We would drive the complete length of Route 6 from Provincetown, Massachusetts to California and then across California to Route 101, go north to Route 20 in Oregon, starting at the coast and returning cross-country to Boston. The Second Hope Longest Roads tour would serve as public awareness for the books, wellness houses in hospitals, and also gather stories for a new book of how people are facing their serious illness using core Second Hope components.

Other Second Hope projects include training medical professionals to provide guidance to patients on how to manage all the stress of an illness beyond the medical cure being attempted.

I would hire a publisher and editor to guide the publication of Second Hope books, as well as my cousin Mark's story of his daughter Lindsey's heart transplant and the Kazmira books. Kazmira is a magical land where imaginary creatures interact with young children to help them deal with issues of growing up. There are 26 magical creatures, one for each letter of the alphabet. The story and creatures have been flowing from my friend Kandi's imagination for over a decade. Perhaps the most important thing I could do near-term is to put a finished copy of her book in her hands.

The foundation for Community Opportunity Conferences would use my hometown, Erie, as a development project. The conference would engage citizens, professionals, and academics in a visionary process we used at National Semiconductor to get consensus on a vision to build toward. The process produces a graphic roadmap that everyone agrees to achieve. The foundation will award grants to nonprofits and private companies to build elements of the vision. Academics could guide the process and do comparison research as well as evaluation of success. All of this would tie in with current community efforts and use existing structures and programs.

Having lived in eight states, I have seen numerous community development efforts fall short of their goals due to insufficient community involvement and a lack of a shared vision with broad support. The graphic visionary maps and process to be used addresses these problems.

A successful model could then be used in other communities with their local foundations providing the funding.

M Wind

The first profit-making organization to be started is what I've been calling "M Wind". M Wind would develop an alternative energy device using magnets to rotate blades that turn a generator to create electricity. The first models would be small house-sized units. Later, commercial scale models could be built. A number of technical challenges exist to harness the repulsion/attraction power of magnets, so this project may take different avenues to develop small-scale energy. Wind could be used to turn the blades and magnets used to turn them when the wind does not blow.

Small solar arrays can also supplement and use the same converter/ storage system.

M Wind is predicated on utilizing small streams of air rather than big rivers of water or air. Multiple units could be used in a home. Think window fan rather than large windmill.

An inventor from Erie, PA invented a radiowave device that targets nanoparticles that have embedded themselves in cancerous tumors. The machine is being tested on large animals now to duplicate the success obtained with small animals. In the process of testing the original device, John Kanzius accidentally discovered that passing radio waves through salt water created a flame that produced heat, which can be converted to electricity. This discovery has not yet been fully tested, but some arrangement could be made to test this discovery within the M Wind alternative energy company.

One Ocean

The next major private venture would be the One Ocean project. It is all one ocean, the only one we have. This was originally conceived as an aquaculture company that would develop a brand image around one ocean. Branded products would carry a message that every purchase also helps to restore wild stocks of endangered fisheries. Recent issues with aquaculture such as torn nets releasing the raised fish and interbreeding with wild stocks, inadequate dispersal of detritus, make this a research project first that might then turn into a nonprofit effort.

The overall goal is to restore the ocean's capacity to enrich the lives of humans, so even if we just slow down the human impact on the ocean, it would be great progress.

This writing is not my first attempt at figuring out what I would do if I were a rich man. The list of twenty-four projects has grown over the years from the initial list of six or seven. There are also nine or ten yellow paper tablets with notes on many of these projects. And I have a spreadsheet from October 4, 2009 that lists the projects and target investment amounts. Organized outlandish musings!

So all this effort is ultimately driven by my life dream, which is a series of dreams that began when I was about 10 years old. The dreams frightened me so badly I was unable to tell anyone about them for decades. I tried several times to tell my wife over those several decades, but each time I was seized by panic and had to stop. I finally was able to tell about the dreams, first to Alan, a therapist who had an office next to mine in Menlo Park, California when I worked at SRI International. This enabled me to tell Kitty about them, which gave her huge insight into many of my decisions and actions. The essential elements of the dream are extraordinary forces set on destroying us and a voice (perhaps God?) telling me that "life as we know it will end unless you take action." The dreams all have nighttime scenes in which total darkness is overtaken by fast-moving spaceships with flashing lights that reveal the shapes of flying trucks, boats, cars, and huge spaceships.

Which all seems rather irrational on the surface, I know. But the number, duration and intensity of these dreams has become a compelling force in my life. Although the threats seemed extraterrestrial due to the many incredible flying spacecraft, it is not hard to see the manifestation of forces here on earth bent on destroying civilization. So, on my walkabout, I'm still compelled to determine if my purpose in life is defined by these dreams and the great visions and ideas that I have imagined (or been given) that have resulted in this list of twenty-four projects.

Or has this life dream and hopeful list just been a long-running delusion of what I have been destined to do? It would be far easier to abandon all these ideas, admit I am retired for good and just figure out how to best use my assets to enjoy my kids, maybe volunteer at the soup kitchen or any other kind of volunteer work. As I write these words, I hate this giving up, this submission to the ordinary. Although I take great pride and comfort in my children and my incredible marriage, I still cannot come to grips with this being my sole legacy. If it were, why was I given all these other ideas and grand visions and compelling drive to do so many other things?

True

Our world is in trouble, our environment is in peril, our governments are ineffectual and in disarray. Our political system in America is laughable, and an abomination of democracy. We need big changes to survive as a species. My array of projects can make a small impact on all this. But more importantly, they can serve as examples and inspiration to others. The Community Opportunity Conference model can be rolled out in hundreds of cities, even small countries.

So, I don't know:

How I could ever stop trying to make this a better world.

How I can begin without large sums of money.

How I can make this a better world by doing simple volunteer work.

I am 65 years old and in excellent health. I'll be in even better health when I lose the second twenty-five pounds! I am thankful for my health, incredibly grateful for my children, glad I have the resources to do this walkabout. My life can be more comfortable and safer than probably eighty percent of the people on earth. So, I should just relax and enjoy it?

I just don't see that happening. So, each day I visualize success, ask God for his help, and buy lottery tickets. Not exactly the greatest formula – what are steps four and five? Steps two and three could do it tomorrow, but that's up to God. What's up to me? I have to find that answer.

Saturday, October 22, 2011

Fort Macon was only several miles from my motel, so I decided to visit it before heading south. Fort Macon was built to protect the town of Beaufort, North Carolina. Fort Macon is a five-sided fort with stone and rock walls that are over four feet thick. It could have easily served as the model of the Pentagon in Washington, D.C. It is surrounded by a moat that could be flooded during an attack. The vaulted rooms inside it were used for living quarters, cooking and dining, as well as munitions storage.

According to the ncparks.gov website, construction of the present fort began in 1826. The fort was garrisoned in 1834. In the 1840s, a system of erosion control was initially engineered by Robert E. Lee, who later became general of the Confederate Army. At the beginning of the Civil War, North Carolina seized the fort from Union forces. The fort was later attacked in 1862, and it fell back into Union hands. For the duration of the war, the fort was a coaling station for U.S. Navy ships.

Fort Macon was a federal prison from 1867 to 1876, garrisoned during the Spanish-American War and closed in 1903. Congress offered the sale of the fort in 1923, and the state purchased the land, making it the second state park. Restored by the Civilian Conservation Corps from 1934-35, the fort was garrisoned for the last time during World War II.

The museum at Fort Macon also has an impressive film on birds. One of the officers stationed there used his spare time to publish a book on birds of the area.

Walking around the fort, it is easy to imagine what combat was like in an era where troops or ships could be seen for miles before they would be in firing range. Preparations could be made to mount a defense while protected behind the solid walls. In modern warfare, a fort like this could be destroyed by a single cruise missile fired by an unseen ship well past the horizon.

Standing on a rampart gazing out to sea, I preferred to imagine the sights and sounds of the 1800s. But, on some level, are people like forts? Do we need to upgrade ourselves to meet new challenges? By virtue of my work as a training consultant, I have been a life-long learner. I worked with subject matter experts to learn what people need to know to do their job. I then combined this with the latest learning technology to develop skills at the highest level. What does this tell me about my walkabout goal of a new infra-structure for my life? Is my ability to learn a more valuable tool than anything I have already learned?

I headed south on Route 58 and Route 24, following the barrier island's roads, which had little traffic this far past the tourist season. Route 24 then bends westward to arc around the huge, sprawling Marine Corps Base Camp Lejeune. On the west side of Camp Lejeune, Route 24 continues west and Route 17 then cuts across the base heading south back toward the ocean. Route 210 then takes you back to another set of barrier islands, where I hoped to find a campsite. Several of them were already closed for the season and the remaining open one was full. But, the ride along the water and the chance to smell the salt air was the best part of the day.

This area around Topsail Beach is less crowded than the Outer Banks further north and has lower rental and hotel prices, but the same great beaches and ocean.

Route 17 continues along the coast until Wilmington, North Carolina, where it continues in a straight line until it meets the ocean again at the border with South Carolina, Since it was dark by the time I reached South Carolina, I opted for a Red Roof Inn on the bypass around the Myrtle Beach area. But, I knew that I had to get back closer to the ocean. The ocean does not often answer any of my questions about life, but it always puts life in perspective.

5. SIT AND PONDER

Sunday, October 23, 2011

The day was sunny and bright and I drove twenty miles south of Myrtle Beach to a campground, where I hoped to enjoy camping on the ocean. My definition of "on the ocean" did not match the available sites. The campsites were all at least 150 yards from the water, with no view of the ocean itself. I could hear the surf, but never see it from the camp. That, along with having to carry everything into the campground, where cars were not allowed, further dampened my enthusiasm. So, I broke my never doubleback rule yet again to go back north to Myrtle Beach and embarked on one of the most pleasurable sequences of the entire walkabout.

Right near the end of the Myrtle Beach boardwalk, I found the Bar Harbor Inn and a $30 a night oceanfront room with a balcony. This was less than half of what I paid last night for a room with a view of a parking lot. I should have thought of the economic law of supply and demand and headed to the ocean the night before. With thousands of oceanfront rooms sitting empty in late October, the prices came down to rock bottom at the hotels that were still open.

Some of the businesses on the boardwalk were closed for the season, but most were still open. Just about everything I needed was within walking distance. The boardwalk became my path to get to the library, the post office, the liquor store, the beach, and the fishing pier. All I needed the car for was a laundromat and the grocery store. If I had a bigger backpack, I could have walked to those places as well. Sounds strange making a case for self-sufficiency in the middle of high rise hotels!

One day as I was driving to the grocery store, I noticed a huge empty parking lot in the middle of town. There were no cars parked in it and cables were strung across the openings into the lot. Perhaps this was overflow parking for the beach, not needed this late in October. Or, was there a NASCAR race track in Myrtle Beach that was only used several times a year? I drove around all four sides of this huge lot and there was no racetrack there. This was only several blocks from the beachfront area and should have been prime, valuable property. Very strange. An empty core of several barren blocks within a hot spot of economic activity did not make any sense.

This scenario was the inverse of the small town survival question that popped up as I drove the highways along the coast. I found a partial answer on a computer at the library. The barren blocks used to be a shopping mall. The mall owner built a new shopping mall closer to the bypass highway a number of years ago and abandoned the old mall to eventual demolition. Still unexplained was why no other developer had undertaken another use of this prime property. This seemed like a prime example of a community that did not have any common vision.

Monday, October 24, 2011.

It is Monday and I've been in Myrtle Beach, for three nights now. My waterfront hotel room with a balcony overlooking the ocean is large and comfortable with a few cracks and stains that are easy to overlook. I have ratcheted up my walking the last two days to eight miles a day and plan to keep increasing it. I can easily eat in the room since it has a refrigerator and microwave.

The sound of the ocean is enormously soothing. I keep the door to the balcony open all evening and sleep with it open. I woke at 5 AM to the cold air and closed it. Several hours later I had an incredible experience, which turned out to be a dream, I think. An arm fell across my body and I immediately knew it was Kitty's. I turned and exclaimed, "It's you!"

She said, "Of course it's me, silly, who else would it be?"

"I, I don't…."

Kitty said "Come on, walk with me, we're going to see the little kids dancing to some jazz musicians. We have the best here."

"Here?"

"Yep. Don't worry; you'll see your parents later. Dad and Ba, too. They'll all be there."

We linked arms and leaned against each other. The warmth and touch of her was overwhelming. My happiness was so intense, something I had not felt in years. But then I grew confused and stopped walking. Then I said "But wait, Kitty, did I cross over?" She replied: "It's okay, sweetie, everything is all right."

"Kitty, I can't stay. I have to go back. We have three children who need…."

With that, I sat bolt upright in bed, gasping for breath. I was in total panic and my heart raced wildly. I felt like I had been drowning and was shot to the surface by some unseen force. It took several minutes to control my breathing and realize where I was – in a hotel room on the ocean. I had been merely asleep and not in a life-threatening situation. As I thought of the abrupt ending, I longed for a comforting word, a little smile, or a hug. But I was not looking at Kitty when I spoke my last words, so it was a complete break from happiness to panic. I know if Kitty had any say in the matter, she would have said, "Of course, Marty, you have to go back. You promised me you would watch over our kids for a long, long, long, long time."

As always, I wish I knew more about dreams. Are they random groupings of our greatest hopes and fears, or was this one sent by Kitty as a reminder of both my major purpose in life and the joy that lies ahead for me?

In any event, it is a significant reminder that I have had and continue to have a wonderful purpose in life, being a husband and a father who has enjoyed a tremendous family and has much more to look forward to with my kids.

I'm remembering a conversation that my son, Cooper, sparked, probably a year or so before Kitty became ill. Cooper was only ten or eleven at the time and he asked us "Do you ever think about why we are even here? What are we supposed to be doing?"

After a few moments, we realized this was a philosophical question, not a geographical question.

I said, "I believe that we are here to make meaning. Of all the creatures on the earth, we are the only ones with complex brains that can examine our actions and explain them to create something meaningful. Consequently, some of us are trying to make improvements and make this a better world. So, I do things like experiment with magnets to develop better energy sources that don't destroy our planet."

Kitty replied, "I've always thought my purpose in life was to stand by and support you, Marty, in whatever you thought was important to do. And raise my kids to become strong, loving people who can also make a difference. So, you and our kids are really my purpose in life."

I was struck then and I am struck now with the utter simplicity and power of those words. I struggled then (and less so now) with allowing myself to take that same viewpoint. While I have always put time and energy into my marriage and our kids, I think I viewed them as my reward, not my purpose. So, if I was a productive, contributing member of society, my reward was having a great time with my family. It took work within the family to make everything happen, but I was maximizing the reward, not fulfilling the purpose.

I have come to accept over the years (even before Kitty died) that one of my major purposes in life was to build a great family. Which continues to reward me and enriches my life.

As I think about it, if everyone had a major purpose to support their spouse or partner and enrich the lives of their children, causing them to want to make a better world, the world would be quite a better place! With Kitty, this was not done in isolation, as she worked full-time her entire adult life. So, her purpose affected her attitude in all that she did and made an impact on many friends, family and work colleagues.

For example, her last job as a Master Scheduler of instructors made a big impact on the instructors, as she worked diligently to give them maximum time with their families. One instructor, Betty, credits Kitty with making her twins possible, because Kitty arranged Betty's schedule around fertility treatment schedules. It was a simple purpose of two goals that drove her success as a wife, mother, friend and colleague.

Tuesday, October 25, 2011

I had the hardest time today figuring out what day of the week it was, which is a good problem to have at times. I decided to stay two more nights in Myrtle Beach, but was surprised to be charged $40 a night instead of $30 which makes me wonder how owners make these decisions. Of course, the clerk did not know anything about why the rate changed and could not figure any way she could charge me my original rate. There are very few people in this hotel, so why did they change the sign out front to a higher price? The net result is that I signed up for two more nights, but I am unlikely to add two or three more. I'll look at prices further south then likely head on.

I wrote long thank you letters to Remlee and Amber for all that they have done to help support Cooper and get him ready for his next big phase of life, going off to college. Both of them have done so much to fill him with love, laughter and confidence. I also wrote Cooper telling him the things I was not able to say in person when we dropped him off to start college.

All three of our children have turned out to be wonderful human beings. Seeing how they have loved each other, nurtured and supported each other gives me the greatest satisfaction – far greater than anything I have experienced through getting my Ph.D. or any career accomplishment. These days, my greatest joy is seeing them all together (plus Steve and John) and having a great time together.

It is hard to explain how this greatest joy is often accompanied (but not always) by such sadness that Kitty is not there to share it. It is not just my sorrow at missing her. It is more a sadness that she is missing out on seeing the wonderful thing that we created together. I know she witnessed much of this in her lifetime and felt the same way that I do. Our family time was the best thing ever. Every dinner together was to be savored and treasured. We often fell asleep laughing together about something one of the kids said during dinner.

We enjoyed together almost four decades of family life that we treasured every day and never took for granted. I am blessed to continue to enjoy all this and I try not to succumb to bewilderment that she is not here to enjoy these wonders she created.

Wednesday, October 26, 2011

Possibilities. They keep cropping up in my mind, although I don't want to think about them yet. I want to continue to empty my mind and think about the life I want to lead. Possibilities soon become constraints or compromises at best. Nonetheless, since they keep popping up in my mind, perhaps if I write them down, they will stop nagging at me and forcing me to think of the practical details of how to pay for my livelihood.

So, in no particular order, here are the things that keep popping up:

> Self publish an electronic version of The Second Hope Approach
> Start giving Second Hope talks to nonprofits
> Write a press release for Second Hope
> Do contract work in training
> Find a related nonprofit organization and volunteer
> Find a nonprofit job
> Ready the Christmas trees for sale
> Sell the tree farm
> Sell my house
> Start trading stocks again

It seems like there should be more, but that's all that's coming up right now! I like the If I Were a Rich Man page a whole lot better!

I just looked through a Myrtle Beach real estate magazine and was struck by the low prices here. A two bedroom, two-bath condominium on the ocean can be purchased for $150,000 to $160,000, which is very cheap by Boston standards. I could sell my house in Kingston, Massachusetts, and buy here for cash. But, then what? I don't know a soul in town. No family here, no friends here. It would be a great place to live on the boardwalk by the ocean, but how can you justify that? So, there are financial solutions to the problem of how to keep a roof over your head, but what do you do by yourself?

Earlier tonight, I saw a shooting star out over the ocean. It was a shorter, but wider track than most shooting stars, nowhere near the size of the one I saw several weeks ago in Cumberland, Maryland.

Thursday, October 27, 2011

This is my sixth night in Myrtle Beach, South Carolina. I only planned to stay for two, but the view from my oceanfront hotel, the Bar Harbor Inn, has been too good to leave. The boardwalk is only 100 yards north of here and I've been able to get in some good walks. I was up to eight miles a day, but backed off today to six miles because of a blister starting on my right heel. I wanted to swim in the ocean, but got nervous yesterday seeing five or six big jellyfish on the beach. None were in front of my hotel, where I planned to swim. I also have thought of going out at night to join the dozens of people walking on the surf with flashlights. But I have not done so yet and wonder why not.

Is this part of my reluctance to engage with other people, my holding back from direct immersion? The same applies to my plan to go have a drink and appetizer at the open deck bar of the fishing pier 200 yards away or at the Land Shark Grill a mile up the boardwalk. I have walked past it five nights in a row without stopping in. So, am I a spectator or a participant in life? It would seem easier to do any of these things if I were with someone, but right now I don't want to be with anyone, except one of my kids.

I called my friend, Mary, tonight and talked for about twenty minutes. She is always fun to talk to and calling her carries no implications. If I didn't call her for three months, she probably wouldn't think anything of it. I told her she was the first person I talked to since leaving Cooper at college almost two weeks ago. Although I talk to her infrequently, she may know more about me and what is going on in my life than anyone, except perhaps my brother, Rodg. I told her I had probably thought about her more than anybody else while I was traveling. I also said I wasn't sure why, except that perhaps she is a safe harbor.

I head out in the morning for Charleston. I plan on just a brief stop in the downtown area and around the southern mansion district and then onto Tybee Island, Georgia to camp for three or four nights. I camped there in the van several times by myself in 1998 and 1999 to get relief from my asthma in Atlanta.

Okay, so I just went down to the car to get a Coke for my nightcap and I decided to go down to the water. I took off my sandals and walked into the surf. It was cool and refreshing! I walked along the surf line for a half-mile north. I could have gone further, but ran into a trove of shells that were hard to walk on. So, I went up to the boardwalk and rinsed off my feet. Walked halfway back in bare feet, but the concrete boardwalk started to act on the blister on my right heel. I put my sandals on and walked back to the hotel, happy to log another mile walking, half of it in the surf.

Friday, October 28, 2011

I was reluctant to leave my high-rise oasis, but it was time to move on. My destination for the day was Tybee Island, but I planned to spend part of the day in Charleston. I had been there several times on business, but had not had time to explore the historic downtown area. I parked at the Visitor's Center and enjoyed the exhibits there, as well as several hours of walking. The waterfront area is now a mix of shipping port activity and tourism. Many of the buildings date to pre-Civil War times. There are horse drawn carriages offering tours and several areas with cobble-stoned roadways or courtyard areas. I am sure my views of the South are unduly influenced by films like Gone With the Wind. But, recent stories about still flying the Confederate flag above the Capitol, or incorporating elements of the Confederate flag into a new South Carolina flag still paint the image of South Carolina hanging on to a time that has long since passed.

I headed south out of Charleston in the middle of the afternoon with the lingering feeling of spending too little time there to really understand the city. Shortly after leaving the city, I pulled into a county park near Ravenal, South Carolina, on Route 17. I planned to have a little picnic lunch. The roadway into the park was a gravel road leading into the forest. It was not looking promising until I suddenly came to a parking lot with a picnic area and a modern visitor center and museum.

I had stumbled into the Caw Caw Interpretive Center. This Center is located on an old rice plantation and tells the story of when rice was king in the south before cotton was king. Like the cotton plantations, the rice plantations were based on slave labor. It is located in an area of vast Lowcountry swamps. The high use of water in rice cultivation ensured an ongoing presence of mosquitoes and other creatures of the swamp. The rice plantations operated in the 18th and 19th centuries. There is still evidence of the earthen dams and canals used, all of which is accessible by miles of hiking trails.

I was about a mile away from the Visitor's Center when I encountered a sign explaining how the rice fields were slowly being reabsorbed into the swamp and marshes. The sign also warned me to be on the lookout for alligators. Maybe I missed a sign at the beginning of the trail, but that would have been useful information to have before setting out! Of course, I may have skipped this beautiful walk through historic grounds altogether.

When I returned to the visitor center at a more rapid pace, I asked a park ranger how often they actually saw alligators. She replied, "I see a mother alligator and her babies out on the Rice Field Trail just about every morning. They sun themselves on the bank of the canal." As I was processing this information, I realized I had just walked that trail. Before I could formulate any suggestions about better signage, the phone rang. The ranger talked briefly and then asked me if I wanted to go see a rattlesnake. Sure, why not! She asked several other people to join us as we walked out of the Center.

We walked through the parking lot and started up a dirt maintenance road. The last group to join us was a family with three young teenagers – two boys and a girl. The three of them ran out ahead of us, ignoring their mother's plea to stay with the group. They stopped about 15 feet away from a snake lying motionless in the middle of the road. The young girl stood behind her brothers and asked if it was dead. Just then, we saw movement inside the snake. The park ranger said it was a diamondback rattler snake and it probably just swallowed a chipmunk or squirrel. She said that the snake would probably stay in the same position for several hours while it digested its meal.

The young girl turned around and walked back to stand next to her parents. Today's biology lesson was over. Alligators, snakes, and chipmunks, oh my.

After viewing more of the exhibits in the Interpretive Center, I returned to Route 17 and headed south to Tybee Island.

When I got to Tybee Island, I was confused by what I saw. Nothing looked familiar. It had been about a dozen years since my last visit, but several landmarks I remembered were simply not there. I consulted my road atlas and decided I had likely confused it with some other beach. So, I had never actually been to Tybee Island! I had to laugh at myself. Was this chasing a false memory or repeating a mistake I had made in the past? Worse yet, was it a harbinger of the aging process? I decided to just laugh it off and not try to examine it too deeply. There were far bigger issues I needed to pay attention to.

I was expecting a beachfront campground, but only found a campground full of huge Recreational Vehicles. The campground bordered a busy road and it was not an acceptable compromise. After a short walk on the beach, I headed to Richmond Hill, Georgia, just past Savannah and found a motel for the night.

Saturday, October 29, 2011

The motel was just off Interstate 95 and I briefly considered getting on it to continue south. But, I have driven that stretch of road half a dozen times and decided to continue on Route 17.

I pulled off a side road to check out the Geechee Kunda museum. I had seen the word Geechee in several storefronts and roadside stands and was curious what it meant. The museum kind of looked like a log cabin and a shack with a sign in front of it. It was closed today, so I didn't really get to find out what was going on there. It is strange driving along this portion of route 17. It parallels I-95 but there's really nothing out here. Just a couple of churches and mobile homes. You wonder what all these churches are doing here, but I don't think I'm going to be driving down any of these side roads today. I have only seen about five cars in the last two hours.

Within an hour of my brief stop at the Geechee Kunda Museum, I came across Fort King George, near Darien, Georgia at the mouth of the Altamaha River. In 1988, through a cooperative effort between the Lower Altamaha Historical Society, and the Georgia Department of Natural Resources, the Fort King George blockhouse was reconstructed. The present blockhouse and surrounding palisades, earthworks and moat are almost an exact duplicate of the Fort as it was in 1721 when the original was built.

Fort King George was a hardship for troops assigned there. A total of 140 officers and soldiers died, mostly from camp diseases such as dysentery and malaria, due to poor sanitation. The soldiers made up *The Independent Company of South Carolina*, an "invalid" company of elderly British Regulars, one hundred in all, sent over from Great Britain. Their suffering was largely caused by their own poor health, and inadequate provisions due to insufficient funding. Problems such as periodic river flooding, indolence, starvation, excessive alcoholism, desertion, enemy threats, and potential mutiny exacerbated hardships at the fort.

The blockhouse, typical of other frontier fortifications in use in colonial America, dominated the fort and offered expansive views of the inland waterways. Fort King George's blockhouse had three floors: the first two floors to serve as repository for ammunition and stores and to provide firing positions for musket-bearing soldiers as well as naval carriage-type cannon; and a third floor for musket defense and observation purposes.

At the time the fort was constructed, there was very little settlement anywhere in the area. Standing in the blockhouse, you can still look out on three sides and see nothing but water and scrub forest. It must have been easy for boredom to overwhelm any sense of purpose and self-discipline, and lead to all the problems the men brought upon themselves. Unlike many other forts I have visited on the walkabout, I found no evidence that the boredom produced any literature of lasting quality. Hearing of this invalid regiment makes me think King George did not really think that France or Spain posed any real threat to British interests in the area. It was not exactly a reward for the troops who had likely served England well for most of their lives. And, with the exception of a few officers, their names are lost to history. Long live the King, indeed!

As I drove away from the fort, I was lost in thought and took a wrong turn. It took me about five minutes to find my way back to the highway. Even though road signs were scarce, there were signs and roads and the car gave me the ability to move several miles very quickly. I had far more resources than the Invalid Regiment in 1721. Exploring the past to find a future is never as straightforward as it ought to be!

6. Camping Out

Although I was heading for Jekyll Island, I decided to stop on St. Simons Island and have lunch at one of the waterfront restaurants. It was a gorgeous sunny day, but I was surprised at the amount of traffic on the narrow island roads. After seeing about thirty cars with Georgia Bulldog flags flying, I realized this was not just sunny day traffic. Today was the traditional rivalry football game between the University of Georgia and the University of Florida. So many Georgia alumni gather every year at St. Simons to watch the game together. Every available parking space was already taken and the restaurants and bars were jammed and I needed a different lunch plan. A granola bar, some grapes, and a bottle of iced tea would have to do. Go Bulldogs!

I made my way through Brunswick, Georgia and got on Route 17 South again. There is a soaring bridge that wings travelers across the mouth of the Brunswick River and the Intracoastal Waterway. Two immense towers hold cables that support the roadway. The bridge itself is beautiful and the views are quite spectacular. As soon as I reached the other side, I found a place to turn around and go over the bridge back to Brunswick. This was too good to only experience it once. Crossing back over it again, I was able to take in the full scope of all the commercial and recreational use of the waterway.

As I turned east on Route 520, a large sign welcomed all alumni of the University of Florida and the University of Georgia to the annual golf outing weekend. Oops, was this going to be a repeat of the throngs at St. Simons Island? I stopped at the Visitor's Center on the Jekyll Island Causeway to find out. Fortunately, I learned that the golf tournament was yesterday and most of the alumni had already left to attend the game. The Visitor's Center staff contacted the campground and secured a spot for me. After almost two months of hauling a tent around, I was actually going to find out if I could set it up by myself!

On the way to the campground, I stopped at a small grocery store and picked up some provisions and ice to last me for several days. I wanted to cook some shrimp over the fire, but could not find any skewers. Instead, I picked up some aluminum pie tins that proved adaptable to cooking just about anything on a campfire. The camp store had well-seasoned firewood that quickly was ready for cooking steak and shrimp.

Despite a few rocks that made it difficult to sink the tent pegs in, the tent went up fairly easily. I settled into a camp chair with a rum punch and watched the steak and shrimp sizzle. The stars came out in a cloudless sky. All I heard was a whisper of wind and a distant roll of waves against the shore. I could see the flicker of a few other campfires, but heard no one. A perfect night.

Sunday, October 30, 2011

I awoke to the chatter of squirrels, glad that I had not bothered to set an alarm. What difference did it make today what time I got up? After getting dressed and having some yogurt, I decided to walk to the fishing pier less than a mile away and look at the ocean. There were two fishermen already on the pier with heavy casting rods. Although the waves were not high, there appeared to be quite a current sweeping from north to south. I decided to figure out where we were in the tidal cycle, so I turned on my phone to check the time. I was surprised to find out it was only 6:45 A.M. I am not an early riser and could not remember when I had been up that early without an alarm clock. I doubt if this is a new trend!

One of the fishermen was from England. He said he came to Jekyll Island every year to fish and he had never been disappointed. He always catches more than enough to feed himself. He releases any fish he knows he is not going to eat that day.

Monday, October 31, 2011

This is my third night of camping at Jekyll Island, Georgia. I woke up this morning to the sound of rain and there were a few more showers until around noon. I managed to get in another bicycle ride, about 17 miles today and 15 miles yesterday. Jekyll Island is not at all commercialized or built-up with high-rise condos like St. Simons or Myrtle Beach. I don't think there's any building higher than three stories so they must have height limitations here and strict zoning. Most of the houses are small ranch homes, most without a garage.

Many of the hotels and restaurants are closed for the season, so it's a good thing I am camping and cooking on the campfire. I tried a baked potato in the campfire coals last night. It came out of the aluminum foil a blackened rock somewhere between a gourd and a geode. I'll try again tonight and cook it less. The two spoonfuls of potato that I got out of it that were not solidified were great.

I've been getting provisions at a little grocery store about 5 miles away. I carry them back in the Crowe Cousin's Reunion green backpack. I rode extra careful today with a bottle of rum in there. Not sure how I would explain to my kids where all the lacerations on my back came from, had I taken a tumble! Coming back each day to the campground you pedal into a 15 to 18 mile an hour headwind coming off the ocean. Fortunately the path veers inland after a mile or so and it becomes easier.

There are limited services on the island, not even a gas station. All the island stores are in two clusters, the first is the historic district where little cottages sell gifts and crafts. The second cluster has the grocery store, a post office, hardware stores, two Real Estate offices, a liquor store, and two gift stores. All these are in separate trailer buildings that look like they could be towed away if a hurricane was coming.

Jekyll Island was originally a winter retreat for the wealthy set in the late 1880s and early 1900s. As their website describes it:

In 1886, Jekyll Island was purchased to become an exclusive winter retreat for America's most elite families, known as the Jekyll Island Club. For more than half a century, the nation's leading families, including the Rockefellers, Morgans, Pulitzers, and Goulds came to Jekyll Island "to secure an escape."

Their homes are described as cottages, but by any common definition, they would be mansions in any other neighborhood. The grouping of these historic buildings represents the only real evidence that this was once the playground of the rich and famous. Even the hotels and condominiums that have been built in recent years are small and ordinary looking, not what one would expect in a resort area. A large portion of the island is undisturbed woodlands with hiking and biking paths that border them. Several businesses rent golf-cart sized electric cars to tour the island.

There are four high quality golf courses on the island, with only a few players in late October in really excellent golf weather. In what seems to be the only departure from a low-key, non-commercialized oceanside resort, there is a water park geared to families. That area was closed due to construction, so it was not possible to see what other facilities were on that corner of the island.

As I sat by my campfire early in the evening, a man and woman stopped by to check out my Smart car. They had never seen one up close and were very puzzled how I could carry enough gear to go camping. When they saw the Massachusetts license plate, they were even more puzzled.

"Did you actually drive down here from Massachusetts?" the man asked.

"Yes, I left the Boston area about two weeks ago, dropped my son off at college in Philadelphia, then drove down the coast, stopping and walking the beaches along the way."

"Wow, it must be nice to have the time to do that," the woman said.

"Yes, I have actually been traveling for most of the last two months. With my son starting college, and my two daughters living on their own, I decided to take a walkabout and see what I should be doing with my life."

"A walkabout?"

"Yeah, it's an Australian term which roughly means drop what you are doing, go take a journey, and figure out what you *should* be doing."

The man replied, "Wow, I hope I can do that someday. It sounds great. What do you think, girl, could we do that someday?"

The woman looked apprehensive. "I don't know. We've been gone from home three days now and I miss the kids a lot already. Have you been talking to your kids while you are away?"

I said, "No, my phone is usually off. I told my friends not to call, and the kids know they can call me anytime, but they haven't."

We talked for a few more minutes, during which they both agreed it would be tough to take several months off from work. I could tell they would continue to talk about it themselves, with the woman finding the problems with it, and the man searching for the right path to make it happen.

As they departed, the man asked, "So, how long are you staying here?"

I said, "I don't know. I decide every morning if I'm going to stay or leave wherever I am."

The woman replied, "Wow, I have never, ever done anything like that!"

I laughed and said, "Yea, it's pretty different for me, too, but I'm really liking it."

After they went back to their own campsite, I thought about the conversation as I cooked my evening meal. I had made an effort to talk with strangers about what I was doing on this trip and have been surprised by the reactions I was getting. Every instance had resulted in more than just idle curiosity about an unusual idea. People's reactions were genuinely positive and inquisitive. Everybody thought it was a great idea, and immediately said they wished they could do it themselves, but even faster found reasons they could not do it.

I had been peppered with questions about using a GPS (no), having a laptop (no), Mapquest directions (no), reservations (no), road atlas (yes), did I miss my home (no), did I miss my kids (some days), have I found my purpose (not yet).

I had known from the beginning that I was doing something out of the mainstream. But, in talking with strangers, I began to sense how really unique my walkabout was. It was not just the logistics of it that fascinated people, it was the freedom to step away from your normal life and face your future. The freedom captivated their interest, but facing the future created a lot of apprehension. I had already turned the corner on that issue and was now intrigued and enthusiastic about facing my future. I thought back to my moments of panic in the springtime when I realized my son's decisions had all been made, but I had been stonewalling my own decisions about my future.

What happened in my own thinking that turned me from apprehensive to excited? That would be useful for other people to know. The answer is courage, but how do you develop it?

I also realize my situation is somewhat different from other people in the Baby Boomer generation, who may not be able to afford the time or money to go on a walkabout for three months. There must be other ways to achieve the same results.

Courage and alternate paths. Figure it out.

On the one hand, I feel very fortunate to be able to do this walkabout. On the other hand, I know that if my wife were still alive, I would be on a different path.

It also struck me that today was Halloween. For the first time in my life, I was not holding a bag out for candy, partying with friends, walking my kids in costumes around the neighborhood, or handing candy out to neighborhood kids. I hoped nobody soaped my windows at home or egged my house!

Tuesday, November 1, 2011

I woke up to an unusual sound right over my head. A small bird had made its way between the rain cover and the mesh roof of the tent. It hopped around on the netting, occasionally catching an edge of a wing in it. I watched it for a few minutes, hoping it would not tear the fabric and started trying to figure out how I could get it out of there without harming it. Suddenly, it turned, hopped down the mesh and flew out the gap it probably came in. Time to move on. I often wonder if these types of random encounters with nature are a learning opportunity that I am missing. Turns out this one was a harbinger of sorts.

I decided to break camp and head south to Florida. As I came off Jekyll Island, I immediately noticed a large number of birds swooping over and under the bridge. Continuing along the Jekyll Island Causeway, the number of birds continued to increase. There appeared to be several types of birds. I drove for miles surrounded by swooping flocks of birds that soared high and dipped low in a frenzy of wings. I slowed down to about 25 miles an hour, fearful that a swarm would smash into me. There were literally thousands of birds in the air. I felt like an intruder in their midst, crashing their party, not even knowing their names. Swallow, sparrow, what do you call yourself? What are you doing here today, when I saw none of you three days ago when I arrived? Hey, look up. That's some kind of raptor circling high in the sky. Watch your back.

The Causeway led me back to Route 17 South again and I headed across the border towards Jacksonville, Florida. I briefly thought about hopping onto Interstate 95 to make my way through the urban sprawl ahead of me. A quick check of my road atlas provided a path using Alternate Route 1 and Route 10 that quickly would take me to the beaches. Route 203 and Route A1A follow the coastline through many beachside communities to St. Augustine, where I found a campsite at Anastasia State Park.

The campsite is a short distance back from the beach, but you can hear the sound of the waves breaking on the shore at night. The sound was not as distinct as my oceanfront room in Myrtle Beach, but it was still a great way to fall asleep. The sand on the beach is very soft and packs down nicely, which made for good walking. You can also rent bicycles to ride on the beach. Each day after taking a five-mile walk through the campground and beach, I thought of renting a bike, but the winds were pretty strong. I saw riders enjoying a ride northward, with grimaces on their faces heading back south into the wind.

I had visited St. Augustine several times before and wanted to experience a few local attractions again. When I arrived at The Alligator Farm, I was surprised to find that they had a zipline that you could ride over the pools of alligators. I had talked with my son several times about finding a zipline attraction to ride together. Riding over alligators was, by far, the most exciting ride I had come across! I picked up a brochure since it was already close to closing time. Sitting by the campfire later that night, I realized that the zipline ticket was about the same amount of money I had spent on food for the last week. Maybe I'll try it some other time!

The hike to the rest room was about a half mile round trip. I must have been still debating the zipline ride/food tradeoff – not exactly an eat or be eaten debate – because I walked off to the rest room and left my soft-sided cooler on the picnic table. When I returned, a camper next to me said he had just chased a big raccoon off my picnic table. I looked and saw my little cooler on the ground. When I picked it up, there was a long tear along the zipper at the top. When I examined the contents, I discovered that the raccoon had stolen some of my cheese. It must have been a European raccoon, because it stole the Asiago cheese and left the Vermont cheddar!

Wednesday, November 2, 2011

I drove back in to St. Augustine to visit the oldest fort in America, Castillo de San Marcos. Construction on it started in 1672 to help protect the port of St. Augustine. It was built out of coquina, which is basically shells that have bonded together over many years into a hard mass, much like limestone. Although it was well distant from the constant wars between France, England, Spain and other European powers during the colonial period, Florida nevertheless became involved because it was part of the trade route that involved Mexico and the Caribbean islands.

Most of the Castillo has been restored and looks much like it did in the 17th century. A reenactment of the firing of a traditional cannon is conducted several times daily, with the same ritual of instructions given in Spanish. While impressive in its grandeur, this fort, like others I had seen, would not serve any military purpose today. Technology has moved on so rapidly that the strengths and capabilities still inherent in the fort made it indefensible in the modern world. This sobering thought may apply to my own strengths and capabilities in facing a different future. Whoosh, time to move on to a different view!

I went to the St. Augustine Lighthouse and climbed the 150 stairs to the top, 140 feet straight up. Many people walked to the top and took a picture and then went straight back down. I stayed at the top for about twenty minutes checking the view in all directions, and talked to a few people, before asking a ranger to take my picture with the ocean in the background. I was struck by how little time most people took to enjoy this spectacular view. Seeing the ocean always inspires me and it was sorely needed after my thoughts at the fort.

Lighthouses have always been inspirational to me. Just seeing them at a distance is a reminder of their basic purpose, which is to protect oceangoing ships from crashing. Their solid structure also evokes strength and grandeur. Climbing the stairs of a lighthouse gives you a sense of the commitment made by the early lighthouse keepers. It was a commitment to a purpose, where there is little margin for error. To me, a lighthouse is a beacon of hope, and the view from the top is always magnificent. Thinking of my next steps forward in life, I heard the Donna Fargo song, *You Can't Be a Beacon if Your Light Don't Shine*. I best remember that.

The downtown area of St. Augustine is a short walk away from the Castillo. A number of the buildings in the general market area are as old as the fort. Several of the streets are closed to vehicular traffic and you can stroll through the lanes and imagine what life was like in the 1700s. Of course, there are no pigs or chickens in the street and the sewer lines are underground now and the young folk are texting on their phones, instead of peeling oranges. But, you can get the general sense of a less hectic time.

Further south of the market area is a unique restaurant that sits on a wharf in the harbor. The Santa Maria Restaurant is located in the heart of historic downtown St. Augustine. It sits out over the Intracoastal Waterway and has great views of Matanzas Bay. In addition to great food at reasonable prices, they give you yesterday's bread to feed the fish while you dine. There are trap doors in the walls next to the table and you can drop pieces of bread down for the fish. Of course, there are also pelicans and a Great Blue Heron or two who feed on the swarms of catfish and mullet that surround the building. Seagulls also frequent the area, so it is often a battle to see who gets each piece of bread that is dropped.

Matanzas Bay also has occasional manatees and dolphins, but I did not see any on this trip. And, I have to admit that feeding the fish was a lot more fun when I was there with my kids. As just about everything is!

Thursday, November 3, 2011

I am watching my campfire at Anastasia State Park in St. Augustine, Florida. It's my third night here and I'm enjoying it immensely. The park includes the ocean beaches, but you cannot see the ocean from the campsite. But you can hear it! I have been walking on the beach and around the campground. Tomorrow, I hope to rent a bike and explore further. The sand is so fine and well packed, it makes for excellent walking and it looks like bicycles cruise along nicely as well.

I decided today that I would stop thinking about why people act the way they do. Back in graduate school, we did some short case studies trying to ascribe motivations to behaviors. We got most of them wrong because the relationship is just too complex. So, I decided then to live my life without judging other people. That was one of the best decisions I ever made! You have no idea how much mental stress I avoided by making that decision! It is occasionally hard to do, but well worth the commitment to a vow.

But, I now realize I have to take it to the next level. Two samples from today help explain this. Here are two examples that irritated me and took me away from thinking about what is important to me.

I went to the library in St. Augustine, Florida to check the weather because earlier it looked like Friday and Saturday it could be raining here. This might impact my camping plans. The man next to me on his computer ignored the many signs about no cell phone use and took a call on his cell phone. I could hear the woman's voice who was calling him as well as his.

"So, you taking a nap, honey?"

"No, I'm at the library."

"Oh, well, you need to call Doug. Not sure what he wants. They want me to work another shift, but I'm already doing 12 hours, so they can forget about that."

"Right, hey, I need to see you as soon as you get back to town."

"Okay, sweetie, should I pick you up at the Marina?"

"Yep, we're going to go look at that house you like this afternoon."

"Perfect! I'll see you soon."

Several minutes later, I finished my computer session and I logged off. As I stood up, I noticed that this 45 to 50-year-old man next to me was perusing women on match.com! What the hell is that about? Was he looking for a backup plan if they could not agree on which house to buy?

Here's the second example of why I have to stop thinking about what other people do with their lives. When I got back to my campsite around 4:15 PM, I unloaded my wood and redistributed the new ice into my little coolers. I noticed a droning noise that was blocking out the sound of the ocean. As I looked around, I realized that the noise was coming from an air conditioner atop a pop-up camper on the site next to me. As I looked closer, I realized no one was there. The camper was not closed in, so I could see through the screen netting. Who is air conditioning the outdoors?

Around 6 PM, a truck pulled onto the site. Two people got out and 10 minutes later they got on bikes to go for a ride. Around 7 PM they returned, built a fire and finally shut off the air conditioning.

Why in the world would people come to a place to enjoy nature, and then leave an air conditioner on in an open trailer for hours? Okay, this really ticks me off, but I have to stop thinking about all the idiots in the world. There are too many of them and there's nothing I can do about it.

Friday, November 4, 2011

Since this might be the last day I was at Anastasia State Park, I was resolved to rent a bike and do that first before my walk. As I walked up to the rental shack it started raining! So, I missed the opportunity of a first bike ride on the beach. Fair weather rider!

I did get a walk in later in the day, but I mainly amused myself with reading in the tent and listening to the rain on the thin fabric.

Saturday, November 5, 2011

The weather forecast included more rain and heavy winds, so I decided to pack up and head further south to my turnaround point, which was at my sister's house in Sebastian, Florida. The coastal road, A1A, winds down through beachside communities and offers multiple places to pull off and watch the waves. I stopped just past

Crescent Beach to go see Ft. Matanzas. Ft. Matanzas guarded the southern approach to St. Augustine, some 14 miles north. It is actually on a small island in the Intracoastal Waterway and is only accessible by boat. I had just missed a boat and decided not to wait an hour for the next one, but there is a small visitor center from which the boat departs. So, I was able to look at pictures of what I was seeing in the distance.

The fort was built of local shellstone called coquina. Lime for the mortar was made by burning oyster shells. I had seen similar construction up close in a historic house on Jekyll Island. Having done some brick and stone work with concrete as mortar, I still have a hard time thinking you can actually build something thirty feet high out of sea shells. And, expect it to sustain bombardment from cannon balls. But, these structures have stood for hundreds of years, so I have to believe it is possible.

My next stop of the day has also seen countless battles, all of them in the last half century. The Daytona International Speedway opened in 1959 and hosts a number of different types of races. There are multiple tracks inside the Speedway that are used for stock car races, sports car races, motorcycle races and even a short one for go-karts. In fact, there is also a 29-acre lake in the middle that has hosted boat races! The size and scope and scale of this place really defies description. In addition to huge parking lots and campgrounds, there is an airport adjacent to the speedway that is used by car owners, drivers, and fans to land right where the action is.

I took a tour that shows you all areas of the Speedway, including the pit area and garages, where millions of dollars of parts are quickly replaced in an average race weekend. Our tour guide apologized for not being able to take our little tour bus on the racetrack, because there were sports cars out there practicing for an upcoming race. But, we did drive close enough to the banked sidewalls for me to get a great sense of the uniqueness of this type of racing. I also intuitively knew our tour bus was never going to ride high around one of those turns!

I sat in one of the 100,000 plus seats in the grandstands and tried to snap a few photos of the sports cars with my cell phone camera. I thought I got a picture of one, but when I checked it, all I could make out was a fence post. OK, stay steady in the moment. I hear a car coming. The sound builds. I see a car and hold the camera steady on a spot in front of me. There is a blur on the screen and the sound fades away. I try panning the phone across the arc of the car and see the car clearly and press the button. Whoosh! Nothing but fence!

So, I gave up on the pictures and watched the cars scream around the track. After awhile I could pick out the distinctive shapes of the Porsches, Ferraris, and Maseratis and realized they each had a distinct sound as well. I am sure each driver garners information out of the sound of their car that none of us would ever notice. Go fast, turn left!

I did have my picture taken in the winner's circle at the end of the tour. I figured it was as close as I was ever going to get to people who made their living driving over two hundred miles an hour. And, nobody sprayed champagne on me.

The rest of my drive was uneventful – all at legal speeds. At New Smyrna Beach, I headed off the barrier island and proceeded south on Route 1. I had driven this road a number of times when we lived on Melbourne Beach from 1987 to 1991. Not much new to see, except some bigger shopping complexes.

I had called my sister earlier in the day to tell her I was coming in a day sooner than I had planned on. She was glad to hear from me, as all she knew was that I was coming sometime this week. That was a reminder that my walkabout schedule did not really matter to me, but it did matter to people I was visiting. It had been three weeks since I had been with family and friends – pretty quick to forget some basic communication protocols.

Just being on the ocean and driving along it for so many days has made me want to live closer to it, so I can hear the surf. I can see the ocean from my house in Kingston, but not hear it. How greedy is that?

7. TURNAROUND

Sunday, November 6 to Wednesday, November 9, 2011

For the next four days, I just hung out with my sister, Kathy, and her son, Brian, when he was not working. We walked the beach or along the Indian River Lagoon each day. It was cooler than usual in October, so I did not get to swim in the ocean.

One day, we visited The Smithsonian Marine Station (SMS) at Fort Pierce. It is a research center specializing in marine biodiversity and ecosystems of Florida. Their research focuses on the Indian River Lagoon and the offshore waters of Florida's east central coast, with comparative studies throughout coastal Florida.

The Station, a facility of the National Museum of Natural History, is part of the Smithsonian Institution in Washington, DC, and serves as a field station that draws scientists and students from the Smithsonian and collaborating institutions around the world to investigate the plants, animals and physical processes in the ocean and Indian River Lagoon. Information uncovered at the Marine Station is published in scientific journals and forms the basis for effective public policies, conservation efforts, and resource management.

As I was looking at the exhibits, including a large aquarium tank full of sea creatures, I thought again of my conversation with friends in Detroit. I had said then that if I had it all to do over again, I might have chosen to study marine biology. So, I could have been working in a place like this, collecting samples, doing dolphin counts, and charting the decline of sea grasses in the Lagoon. I looked at the charts of data that represented years of work and realized I had made a better choice to study educational psychology and train future teachers and workers in business and manufacturing industries. My career as a trainer challenged me to learn concrete job skills across fields like computers, semiconductors, pharmaceuticals, biotechnology, accounting, banking and manufacturing. My work spanned marketing, sales, engineering, business practices, and customer service. I think my view of marine biology may have focused on the exciting part of diving on coral reefs every day and not wading in the water doing repetitive tasks every day. But, does any college student have an accurate picture of what working in their chosen field is like? This is a good reminder to engage in some serious discussion with Cooper about the jobs that a major in mathematics and economics will qualify him for.

Despite my misgivings about the more mundane tasks of marine biology, my abiding interest in environmental causes and the huge impact of the ocean on our environment leads me to think I am not done investigating marine biology. Beyond donating small amounts of money to marine groups every year, there must be something more direct I can do to help the oceans. My varied skill set could be applied in many ways throughout the larger issues without necessarily having the detailed subject matter expertise that a degree in marine biology would afford.

In any event, the first step is to do a better job of not letting other issues keep me from participating in the International Coastal Cleanup every September. I missed the last two years due to a wedding and my walkabout. I was never that far from the ocean on my walkabout and I could have participated wherever I was that day with a little forethought. Step by step.

I had realized too late in my stay in Florida that there was a museum nearby that documented the history and exploits of the Navy Seals Underwater Demolition Team. Although that job relies heavily on scuba diving, I hold no illusions that I would have ever wanted to do something like that. I also have no illusions that I could have ever qualified for this elite unit! But, I will plan to visit the Museum on my next trip to Florida.

Thursday, November 10, 2011

It was a hot, sunny day and I briefly thought of delaying my departure for Atlanta, so I could take a swim in the ocean. But, I wanted to do the drive in two days on the state highways and have time to stop along the way. My first planned stop was a candy store in Melbourne, Florida. It was not just for candy.

I deliberately set out to engage a strange woman in a conversation. When I was in Florida in September, Kathy and I went to a candy store in Melbourne to buy some chocolate covered potato chips. We first came across the chips when we lived there and bought Remlee a car for her 16th birthday. The little red Ford Festiva came with a box of the chips. We've been hooked on them ever since.

The woman in the store had caught my eye, as she was good looking, trim, confident and friendly. On that visit, I said relatively little to her, but I did remember her. So, on today's visit I spoke more.

"So, is it too soon to buy the chocolate covered chips for Christmas?"

"Well, I don't think so. It's almost Thanksgiving."

She walked over to where I stood looking at the chips. She picked up a box and pointed out the expiration date was January 11, 2012. I looked at her hand and again confirmed she wore no wedding ring. So I said, "Okay, that solves one problem. Now I have to figure out how many boxes I can fit in my Smart car and still have room to fit in my son's gear when I pick him up for Thanksgiving."

She looked out the window and said, "Is that your Smart car? I've never seen one up close." She walked toward the door and I followed her. She said, "I'm going to take a closer look." We walked outside and I opened the car door for her and said, "Take a good look."

"Okay, that's roomier than I pictured."

"The passenger compartment is about the same as a small sedan. So there is plenty of room."

"But, nothing behind you."

"I have a tent and camping gear in there. It does hold quite a lot."

"But, no other passengers."

"Right, it's just for two. I've put a lot of miles on it the last two months."

"Really. Where have you been?"

"I started near Boston, dropped my son at his college in Philadelphia, went to Atlantic City, and I have been driving down the coast and walking beaches from New Jersey to Florida."

"Wow, that's great to have that much time."

"Well, for almost 40 years, I went to bed and woke up thinking about what do the kids and my wife need from me today. My wife passed away almost seven years ago."

"I'm sorry."

"Now, my last child is off to college and I decided to do some traveling and figure out what the new infrastructure of my life should be."

"What a neat thing to do. Most times we never get a chance to plot things out."

"I know. I brought along a lot of music, thinking it would be good to hear as I drove. But I haven't listened to any of it. I'm just enjoying the silence."

"You know, you're lucky to have so much quiet time. Even just having a three-day weekend to yourself is a rare thing."

"I know and I feel blessed that I am able to do this. It's like creating a vacuum and seeing what gets pulled in."

"It sounds kind of new-age like, but I think not. You're really going to figure out what you should be doing. I have grandkids and I think that's going to be the next step in my path."

I nodded and smiled at her. She said, "So, any insights yet?" I laughed and said, "I'm working on that. I feel it coming in. I told my sister the other day that the kids and a few other people would be asking me that question soon. And I don't know if I'll have a plan or a cover story to talk about."

She laughed and said, "But you'll be ready."

"I will."

Out of the corner of my eye, I saw several other people about to open the door to the store. I had already selected and paid for the boxes I wanted as we talked. I extended my hand and said, "I'm Marty Crowe." She shook my hand and said, "I'm Phyllis."

"It's been a pleasure, Phyllis."

As she walked away to help the other customers, she said, "I'll keep you in my prayers."

"Thank you."

"Good luck with finishing your plan…. Or your cover story."

As I walked towards the door, I waved and said, "It'll be a plan."

She laughed and said, "Okay, a plan then."

As I drove towards Orlando after this interchange, I thought about Phyllis and hoped I would see her again. I also thought of how to turn myself from a friendly customer to a friend or what....

I could e-mail her at the store, call or send a note – got the chips safely to Boston. So, was this practice or what? The vacuum pulled something in. Thank you, Phyllis.

I left Melbourne feeling good that I had taken the chance to have a conversation with a stranger, which was part of my plan to be a little more outgoing. I slowly made my way through Kissimmee and Orlando on State highways 192 and 441. For many miles these roads have every retail business imaginable. My progress was quite slow and I debated about getting onto an Interstate highway. But I decided to stick with the congestion and see what I could learn. I quickly learned that many businesses were aggressively seeking customers. It was not just signs in windows announcing sales. It was carnival style hawkers on the sidewalks and medians holding signs announcing discounts and specials of the day.

Some of these hawkers were in costumes and some had body paint and painted faces. There were young girls in tight short shorts and bathing suit tops. There was a man on stilts and one in a wheelchair. They were trying to pull us into their restaurant, jewelry store, furniture store, oil change place, car wash, or appliance outlet. I rolled down the windows to hear what they were saying as they waved their placards at us.

"Only $15 for an oil change. We have an open bay."

"Free dessert with every meal!"

"Bring your gold in. We buy it all."

"Wash your car today and get a half price coupon for the next time."

"Nice car, mister. Stop in and check out our sales."

Suddenly, the carnival midway had arrived on Main Street, USA! I had seen similar people occasionally on the trip, but not a gauntlet of several miles of them. I wonder how the economics of that works. Are these hawkers on the payroll or working on commission? Are they jobless people offering to bring in new business in hopes of getting a job with the company? What is going on here? How long before I find myself standing somewhere with a sign? Specials on hope and purpose today!

I soon was out of the commercial area and was able to relax and enjoy the scenery heading to Ocala on Route 27. Ocala is horse farm country with a few rolling hills amidst the flat pastureland. The rest of the day heading north on Route 27 and 41 was uneventful. Those roads roughly parallel Interstate 75, but I resisted the urge to leave the slower road.

Just after dusk, I stopped at a small roadside motel and got a room. Although I had been staying in mostly cheaper hotels on this trip, this was the first one I would never go back to. It was one of only two on the trip where you still used a room key instead of a magnetic card. The doorknob was close to falling off and the security chain no longer stayed in the bent slot. A sign on the exterior wall said, "No loitering after dark. Trespassers will be arrested." The air conditioning was very loud and made strange crackling noises. I don't get too creeped out by older hotel rooms in need of paint or other maintenance, but the accumulation of issues here did make me uncomfortable.

8. Cotton Fields Forever

11/11/11

Quite an auspicious date! It's morning and I'll check out at 11 to drive to Atlanta. There's that number again!

Although I am avoiding summarizing the walkabout or coming to any grand conclusions, it feels like some big brush strokes are happening.

I want to be healthy enough for a long time to enjoy and support my kids. So, I have to get to an optimum weight and keep exercising. I have to stabilize my finances, probably by selling the house and living in a cheaper place.

Since my top priority is my kids, I need to do that on the South Shore of Boston, since they are tied to it by jobs and friends (and each other!). I also want to continue or restart my Second Hope project, so I may have to self publish it electronically and get over my reluctance to reach out through calls, writing letters, and engaging with other people. And, in 2012, I will get the Christmas tree farm in shape and evaluate doing wholesale sales off of it, a cut-your-own tree operation, and/or sell the lot to the new owner next door who has expressed an interest in owning it.

I had a bottle of apple juice and a granola bar for my breakfast and headed north on U.S. Highway 41. After driving for several miles, I realized that my audio recorder was in the back of the car, so I pulled into a store parking lot to retrieve it.

Keep God's Commandments

The pickup truck that was parked next to me had three teenagers or young adults in their early 20s. The windows were open and I noticed the music that was playing was this god-awful rap music by some young singer. I have no idea who the singer was, but it had all kinds of profanity in it as well as the mistreatment of women or anybody else that happened across this singer's path.

There were two women and one man in the pickup truck. They all lit up cigarettes and were bobbing their heads to the music. And I'm thinking if this is their only contact with civilization down here in the middle of nowhere Georgia, these young kids are in trouble. But then I thought there is no way. This is not civilization we're talking about in this song.

As I pulled out of the parking lot I saw a bumper sticker on their pickup truck. It read Keep God's Commandments. Should I still be worried about these three kids in the south of Georgia? Talk about culture clash. Who is going to win out?

As I got to the traffic light heading out of town there was a one legged woman trying to make her way across the intersection on crutches. I stopped to let her pass and she kept trucking up the sidewalk at a very high rate of speed. I'm not sure what her mission of the day was but she was hell-bent on getting there.

Driving up Highway 41 again past the Georgia Motor Speedway. Looks like they were getting ready for a weekend race there, judging by the number of pickup trucks with trailers pulling onto the lot.

There are lots of cotton fields around here and I'm trying to figure out what the difference is in them because so many of them look different.

Some of them obviously look like they have been picked. Other fields look like they were actually cultivated and now everything has been cut down on them and the soil is tilled again.

Others are full of cotton in the bushes that they grow on. Some have just leaves on them and some have cotton in the leaves, so I don't know if these are different stages of growth or what.

One field has very short bushes on it with very little cotton on the bushes. It may be a younger stage of growth but I have no idea if that's late cotton for this year or if it's just a cotton field that has to take a couple years to get large enough to be productive.

Several other fields had huge blocks of cotton in them about the size of a tractor-trailer and several of these big blocks of cotton had blue tarps over the top of them but they only went about halfway down. I guess the tarps protect the bale from getting water-soaked and if rain hits the lower portion, it just rolls down, rather than sinking in.

As I drive along I see many bolls of cotton that have made their way from the field to the side of the road. I'm not sure what happens to all of these. In some places it's so thick you could go through and scoop it up with shovels. I don't know what you call all this. Is this the snowy white litter of the South?

It makes me wonder how many pairs of pants and shirts and blouses can be made out of that huge block of cotton in the field. We all wear cotton and see it and use it every day of our lives, but I realize I know so little about the whole process. How can something be so pervasive in our lives and we know so little about it? We need Mark Kurlansky to write a book about cotton, similar to his books on salt and cod, which explain the historical and economic development of some very basic foods. Cotton certainly has had a similar pervasive impact over hundreds of years, if not longer.

These little towns I've been driving through typically have a convenience store and a hardware store and a gas station but so many other buildings are all boarded up. Many hotels have not been occupied in years, as evidenced by the caved-in roof and the broken windows in the rooms.

Most of these towns also have a bar and a church or two and sometimes a bowling alley.

You can really tell the impact the opening of the Interstates had on all these small towns that used to be on the main highway. Now the traffic no longer comes through them and the businesses are boarded up because everybody was zooming by on the Interstate and there are not enough local people to support the storefronts any longer.

Through the 50s, 60s and early 70s, some of the small towns just started disappearing and people moved elsewhere, but there are still some people around trying to make a living in these places. They're going somewhere else to work because you don't see very many commercial enterprises along these state highways.

Every once in a while you'll see a big chemical company or a pharmaceutical company out in the middle of nowhere, far away from any large cities. I wonder how they made the decision to locate them out here, but somehow they get their hundreds or thousands of employees, apparently at cheap labor prices.

Many of these places that I drive through, you do see lots of litter along the highway but there are other small towns where you see none. Is this a function of local budgets or community pride?

I just passed a peanut processing facility, coming out of Cordell, Georgia. It is a huge complex with all different kinds of machinery there and huge satellite buildings. There were a dozen round devices similar to the Christmas tree balers I see up north. Not sure if this strips peanuts off the vines. The devices are all on wheels, so they could easily be towed to the peanut fields to strip vines there.

About half a mile later I passed a complex that processed cotton as well as peanuts. It must have had about thirty of those huge trailer size blocks of cotton sitting outside and a lot of different trailers for all kinds of stuff. Then there was another field with eight to ten trailer-size rectangles of cotton. Without the blue tarps on them, they looked like a stack of giant sugar cubes.

As I looked at the logistics of the whole process of cotton from plants to clothing, it was mind-boggling to think of all the various steps involved. A farmer plants cotton, fertilizes it, weeds the field, and harvests the cotton into compressed bales. The cotton bales are aggregated, and shipped to a wholesaler who sells to a processor who spins the cotton into thread. The thread is then woven into various types of cloth, dyed, cut and sewed into various articles of clothing. The clothing is sold from the manufacturer through a distributor to retail stores. The retail stores receive racks, boxes, or bins of clothing and unpack them, add price tags as needed, and put the clothes on display to sell them to all of us. I am sure I have missed a few steps in the process!

From cottonseed to cotton tee shirt, how many people have touched the cotton and driven it hundreds, if not thousands of miles, before it shows up in my local store. Then, I put it back on the rack because I don't want to pay ten dollars for it!

9. OLD GUYS NAPPING

As I neared Macon, Georgia, I decided to get onto Interstate 75 to try to get to my destination in Marietta, before the Atlanta Friday evening rush hour traffic got too bad. But, it got jammed up earlier than when I lived in the area from 1995 to 2000. So, before I got to Interstate 285, the beltway around the city, I was doing the slow-and-go routine that I had not experienced in a long time. Although rush hour traffic does give you more time to think about things, it must cause some cognitive dysfunction, because I missed at least three turns that I should have remembered.

Although we lived in Roswell on the north side of Atlanta, I had become very familiar with Marietta on the West side of Atlanta from visiting friends there and taking my daughter, Amber, to many gyms in the area for volleyball practices and games. She played both high school and club volleyball for four years around Atlanta. I could have blamed my confusion on new buildings in the last decade, but the reality was I had confused several road names and their geographical orientation. When I found myself too far west of Marietta with no familiar sights, I called my friend to have him reel me in.

I'm not sure if it's really a guy thing to never ask for directions, but I am occasionally chagrined when I have to ask! Nonetheless, I was within about ten minutes of my destination when I sent out the SOS. It does make me wonder how the early pioneers ever found their way anywhere without roads, maps, GPS, and cell phones. Do you suppose there were early settlers who sent letters back east, saying they had settled in Kansas, but they were really in Nebraska? And, how did those letters get back east?

My host in Marietta was Tex, who has been my friend since high school. He lives with a friend, Nancy, who only knows him as Jim. I forget who tagged him with his nickname, but as soon as you see him walk, you know the name fits. One of the first things we did after opening a beer was to call another high school buddy via Skype. Ric was now living in St. Petersburg, Florida, with his wife, Myra. Ric had suffered a stroke and a heart attack in fairly quick succession about a year prior. I had been in touch with him by email since then, but had not heard his voice.

Tex had gone down to help during the health scare and had been giving us updates. I wasn't sure what to expect. Having to relearn how to walk and how to talk had defined Ric's life for the past year. Nonetheless, I was delighted to see the same old irreverent spirit in Ric. His zingers were only a half second slower than usual, but just as pointed. Our hometown, Erie, was a cultural melting pot built around ethnic churches and neighborhoods. But, our high school, Cathedral Prep, was a private Catholic school for boys, which drew from all over the city and all of its ethnic groups.

So, it was not too long into our Skype call before the ethnic razzing began. I am Irish, Tex is Italian, and Ric has Russian and Polish heritage –although other terms were used in our rollicking conversation! The other terms we used are no longer politically correct, but we thought nothing of using them in the 1960s. In fact, we saw nothing wrong with using them because we never used them in a derogatory manner. They were just descriptors and there was no hierarchy or superiority involved and no one ever took offense. Our Catholic parishes reflected the predominant immigrant group in the neighborhood. So, St. Patrick's was predominantly Irish and St. Stanislaus was predominantly Polish. I can remember lots of guys fighting about things in grade school and high school, but it was never about our ethnic background and the nicknames used for them.

After finishing our conversation and saying goodbye to Ric, I told Tex I hoped nobody had hacked our conversation and recorded it, as none of us could have coached Little League again, let alone run for public office. We both laughed and agreed it meant nothing now amongst old friends, just as it meant nothing back in the 1960s. But, it does mean something now in public conversation, which is a good thing. Apparently, not everyone used those nicknames in the openhearted fashion we did.

After dinner, we talked about my walkabout as a turning point with many options. Tex told a story of a turning point in his career that almost did not happen. He had interviewed for a new position and heard through a friend that night that the interview likely left him short of being offered the job. The friend told him that he seemed to have all the right ingredients, but not in the right proportions. So, Tex sat in his hotel room that night and wrote down every question and what his answers were. He then reconstructed his answers to better demonstrate the depth and breadth of his capabilities.

The next morning, he called the hiring manager and asked if he could meet with him again because he realized he had not come across as well as he could have. The manager agreed to a second meeting and Tex led him through the process with a much-improved performance. Tex was offered the new position and began his career in sales. Since then, he has looked at his sales presentations much like a baker looks at a cake. You have to have the right proportions of all the necessary ingredients in order for the cake to come out right.

Saturday, November 12, 2011

Saturday morning was a crisp, sunny fall day. Fall foliage in Atlanta is not as stunning as in New England. Part of the reason is that there are fewer hardwood trees. The Atlanta area is embedded in the Piedmont Plateau, which is dominated by pine trees. So you have to look around harder for the hardwood trees. We did find some clusters of them as we drove around, mostly seeing muted red leaves and a few predominantly yellow trees.

Tex drove us around the old downtown area of Roswell, near where I used to work. A lot had changed in the area in the last ten years. The town leaders of Roswell and several private developers had decided to counteract the suburban sprawl of strip plazas and acres of parking lots by reviving the old downtown area. Ten years ago, when I left Roswell, there were maybe seven or eight businesses downtown. Now, in November of 2011, there were around twenty-five and people were out walking, shopping, and eating at sidewalk cafes. By fixing sidewalks, putting in decorative lighting, and adding some creative stores, the ambience had changed from a few struggling businesses to a friendly community.

Several blocks south of downtown, we had trouble finding my old office building, due to some condominiums erected next door. My prior office was called The Old Bricks. It was similar to row houses, built as housing for the original workers at a cotton mill next door. They were the first built in the South, and possibly, the United States, as apartments for rent. The mill became a leading manufacturer of blankets and uniforms used by the Confederate Army. Union forces burned the Mill in July 1864, but the Bricks were spared to use as housing for officers and as a hospital. By this time, all the men were off fighting in the war and the workers were mainly women. About 400 women were arrested and put on trains and sent north to a prison in Kentucky. Most of them never returned.

The local legend was that The Bricks were haunted. One ghost was said to be a Confederate soldier still looking for his wife. Several of my fellow employees claimed to hear footsteps when they were alone in the building, or catch a quick glimpse of a man in a long gray coat. But I never heard or saw anything out of the ordinary in my five years there.

Today, The Old Bricks have been converted to upscale condominiums, with other condominiums built nearby. The new condominiums were built in a style to match the architecture of the Civil War period, so there is now an artful blending of historic places with new residential and office areas.

We found a local place nearby to have lunch. I usually go for the most unusual items on the menu and got fried green tomatoes and sausage chicken wings. Both were excellent choices. Near as I could figure, a piece of sausage was connected to a chicken wing bone and broiled or fried. OK, so it was delicious, but indescribable.

When we returned to Tex's house after lunch, Nancy was off with one of her children, so Tex and I settled into easy chairs to watch the University of Georgia football game with Auburn. Despite the usual college hoopla of big rivalries and an exciting game, both Tex and I were soon asleep. The final score of Georgia 45 and Auburn 7 definitely put it in the "snooze fest" category, as we so ably demonstrated.

I awoke shortly before Tex did and had this funny image of a dozen old guys, all high school buddies, napping on couches. We were all buried in quilts and snoring away, except for one wild-eyed beer drinker who kept shouting, "Go, Bulldogs!"

Rather than ask Tex to guess who this guy was going to be in twenty years (or, maybe five!), I decided to go back in time, not forward. So, I said, "Tex, I had this conversation with Tom, when I saw him in Detroit several months ago. We had this big group of friends in high school that hung out together. Sometimes, people drifted in or out of the group. But, who was the leader of the pack?"

Tex replied, "I never really thought about that. Buddha Bob was definitely the mission leader. He planned all those missions."

"OK, that was one piece of it. Bob was definitely the mission commander. But, there was a lot more going on."

"Well, Jim had a lot of influence on some of us. He organized the Sin House apartment where a bunch of us lived."

"Well, that was after high school. Who was the Leader of the Pack during high school?"

I then said, "Tom and I got into this conversation because he said he never felt like a leader in high school, but then he got into sales after college and became president of a manufacturing company. He never saw that coming."

Tex replied, "I'm not surprised at that. I remember Tom as a leader sometimes."

I said, "I took a few leadership roles for school dances, but as far as the group of guys went, I was not leading. But, nobody was ever sitting around waiting for just one guy to come up with a plan for the weekend."

We talked about several other suspects, like O.B., and Detz, but did not come up with a definitive answer.

Later that night, we went out for dinner with Nancy. We reprised some of our conversation with her and told a few stories about high school. When we asked her if there was a leader of her pack, she talked about a different kind of experience with a few good friends. She recalled good times, but with a smaller group of several good friends. There was no larger group that assembled except for occasional dances. Our pack in high school had a core group of about a dozen, most of who still keep in touch today. But, it could also grow to thirty or more at different times of the year, probably related to cycles of fall or spring sports.

Over the years, I have come to appreciate that my high school years were different from many people's experiences. It was unique in being part of a large, but changing group, and also unique in that so many of us are still in touch. It seems more common today for people to have friends from college they still see, but very few, if any, from high school. Probably 90% of the real friends I have had in my life are my high school friends. The sobering part of that thought is we are all the leading edge of the baby boomer generation, and we have lost a few of the best of us in a trend that is unlikely to abate.

Sunday, November 13, 2011

I awoke to another crisp, sunny Fall day in the south, ready to continue north on my walkabout. After breakfast, Tex gave me a big hug before I walked out the door. He said he was going to think some more about the leader of the pack question. He thought it was interesting that none of us had come up with a definitive answer.

I rolled down my car window to wave as I pulled away. Tex ambled down the stairs and said, "Any given night!"

I said, "OK, what does that mean?"

Tex replied, "Any given night, any one of us was the leader of the pack."

"I like it. Any given night. Catch you later, brother."

As I drove away, I could hear Frankie Valli singing – "Oh, what a night. It was late December, back in 63. I remember, what a night."

The Old Neighborhood

Roswell, Georgia was the last place my family lived before moving to our current location in Kingston. Driving around the places that occupied our lives so well for almost five years was a mostly pleasurable experience. I drove again by the Old Bricks, wondering how long I might have continued to be a partner in the training business there, if I had not developed asthma. In the Fall of 1998, I became very ill with what I thought was a flu bug. Still feeling bad after a week, I went to see my doctor. Several prescriptions did nothing to help and I began to see some specialists. I was soon diagnosed with asthma, something I had never experienced in my life before.

I soon learned that the Atlanta area was becoming the American leader in adult-onset asthma. There was something in the air there that was poisoning my lungs. After several weeks of using two different inhalers, I had some relief, but could not shake the fatigue I was experiencing. It got to the point where I could not stay awake or walk farther than 100 yards without stopping. My legs trembled with weakness and it was hard to raise my arms to get dressed. I decided that I could no longer work, but had to devote my time to getting well. My business partner, Bob, graciously offered to buy out my share of the business.

I kept going to several doctors and gave dozens of blood samples as the doctors looked in many directions. Finally, after about six miserable weeks, the doctor called and said, "Stop using the Azmacort inhaler. Your muscle enzyme levels are about five times as high as they should be. Your body is not processing the steroid in it. It's all being retained in your muscles, which is what is making you weak."

I was so glad to hear some news I could take action on that I did not express surprise that steroids were making me weak. My only notion about steroids was that body builders used them to bulk up their muscles.

So, now something in the air was poisoning my lungs and the medicine for it was poisoning my muscles! Pretty lousy scenario no matter how you look at it. My pulmonary specialist provided a different inhaler prescription and I stopped using the one containing steroids. Within about two weeks, I was free of the muscle weakness and fatigue. But, I still had debilitating asthma, which the inhalers could not always control.

The doctor told me my best course of action was to move to the desert or to the ocean. The natural choice for all of us was to move to the ocean, but my daughter still had two more years of high school to go. Having uprooted her older sister in the middle of high school, I knew how wrenching that could be. So, we decided to tough it out. I was able to do some contract work for my old company, but I wound up having to leave every three to four weeks when my asthma got too bad. I would drive to the Georgia coast and camp for three or four days, or drive eight hours to my sister's house in Florida. I traveled several other places for work or pleasure. In every case, no matter where I went, my lungs improved in two days and the asthma attacks went away. Further evidence there was something in the Atlanta air that made me very sick.

My daughter, Amber, graduated in June 2000, and committed to play volleyball at Bridgewater State College in Massachusetts. This made it easy for us to not only move to the ocean, but also to return to Massachusetts where we had lived from 1977 to 1987.

We left the Atlanta area in August of 2000 and I never touched an inhaler again. If I had not developed asthma, I might still be driving to work at The Old Bricks in Roswell, for all I know. Sometimes, we choose our turning points in life, but not every time.

I drove across town to the other side of Roswell. There were several new shopping plazas along the main road, Holcomb Bridge Road. But, enough had remained the same over the last decade so that it was easy to find the places that we had frequented for five years from 1995 to 2000. I sent some pictures by phone to my kids – places they would remember, like Cooper's after school program and the Chick-Fil-A where Amber got her first job when she was fourteen. I can still remember the first time she served us our order, just as I remember seeing her older sister working in Jimmy Joe's BBQ Restaurant in Melbourne Beach, Florida. So, both my daughters got their food service ticket punched, just as most American teenagers do to gain entry to the working world.

I also sent a picture of Amber's Centennial High School and thought of all the adventures we all had following her volleyball team around to games and tournaments, including their second place finish in the state championships. Driving into our old neighborhood was interesting, as none of the street names seemed familiar, but I made every turn automatically, just as I had done over a decade ago. It was almost like muscle memory took over as my arms turned the wheel at the right corners. Driving past our old house, I imagined where each room was, and thought of the 12 foot Christmas trees we had in the living room. This was by far the biggest house we had lived in, but we made use of every room fully for different purposes, including two offices. We even had a room in the lower level that we called the box room. The box room contained our luggage, computer and appliance boxes, plus folded moving boxes that our history showed we would use again. Because it had no windows, it was also our tornado shelter room, which we had to use twice when tornadoes hit less than a mile away. Too close for comfort.

As I surveyed the Roswell landscape driving through, dozens of memories came back of restaurants we ate in, places we shopped, the movie theater, the bookstore, the car repair places, and our friend's houses. Each of those places is now supplanted by the current set in a town ten states to the northeast. Having lived in eight states, we are used to this wholesale replacement of suppliers of the daily logistics of life. Each place that we have lived, we wind up with a couple of friends that we still stay in touch with, but the other 90% fade away. That seems to be a self-selection process that is beyond our control. Each move has been predicated by some job change, either Kitty's or mine. I used to joke that we were just migrant workers following the technology crops. How else would you explain it?

I left the Atlanta area filled with good memories. I headed east and circled around the University of Georgia in Athens to head north on U.S. Route 29, which takes you through the small town of Royston, Georgia. It is impossible to drive through Royston without discovering that it is the hometown of Ty Cobb, arguably one of the three best men to ever play the game of baseball. I stopped at the Ty Cobb Museum, but it was closed, this being a Sunday. Sundays seem like a good day to have a museum open, but what do I know? I'm just a guy on a walkabout.

The Hospital is also named the Ty Cobb Hospital, and several other places display his name. Even the police here have Home of Ty Cobb on the doors of their police cars. Everyone is using Ty Cobb as a reason to be proud of Royston, GA. That makes sense to me. My son, Cooper, is a baseball card collector and could tell us the value of the last Ty Cobb card to be sold. I believe it is a seven figure number. When I collected baseball cards in the 50s and 60s, I knew then that a Ty Cobb card was worth a king's ransom, so today it may be the annual budget of some small nation.

My own baseball card collection was contained in three cigar boxes that are lost to posterity somewhere. Losing track of them was quite foolish, because some of my Roger Maris, Mickey Mantle, or Bob Feller cards could have made a decent contribution to the kid's college funds.

Shortly after leaving Royston, I made a stop for a picnic lunch at the state border with South Carolina. Hartwell Dam is an impressive structure that serves as the center point of water recreation areas along the Savannah River. I continued through South Carolina on Route 29, except for the distance between Greenville and Spartanburg. Shortly after Spartanburg, I returned to Route 29 and found the Cowpens National Battlefield. Cowpens was a decisive battlefield ground in 1781 where American forces under Daniel Morgan defeated the British under Banastre Tarleton. This kept the British from taking control of the South. Today, the battlefield looks much like it did several days before the battle, serene and peaceful. But, for a few days over 230 years ago, the fate of an emerging nation was contested in a bloody, hand-to-hand battle. What generation of children will grow up in a world where the only battlefields are historical parks, not the streets they travel to go to school?

10. Heading Home

Monday, November 14, 2011

I am now in Charlotte at a Rodeway Inn for two nights. I spent Friday night, Saturday, and Sunday morning with Tex and his friend, Nancy. It was a great relaxing fun time with chances to talk about my walkabout. Saying something out loud gives it a different tenor than the privacy of your own mind. Tex was good about asking for clarification or pushing me to look at things slightly differently. It's like a good tennis match when you loosen up first, then gradually increase the pace to push yourself and get better as you try different speeds and angles to see how intense you can make it.

Certain things are becoming clear to me. Perhaps these are guiding principles of the walkabout:

Surviving is not enough. I want to thrive.

Thriving is achievement and accomplishing worthwhile things every day in all facets of life.

I need to establish financial stability. This could mean selling my house.

My number one priority is my children, so I have to live near them.

I need to get Second Hope into the light.

I need to develop a Return On Investment plan for the tree farm.

Goals from logbook:

Enjoy and support my kids
Good health/diet
Exercise
Be productive daily
Be productive long-term
Live without clutter
Go to sleep with the sound of waves

Second Hope task list

Print and review e-mails from Rodg
Research e-publishing
Identify e-publishing service company
Finish diet chapter
Edit complete manuscript
Install video on Second Hope website
Install video on other sites
Write press release
Send letters to organizations
Fix Second Hope reporting/Corporation

Christmas Tree Farm task list

Get Brush hog running
Buy Weed Wacker
Cut down the grass
Prune trees
Shear trees
Assess wholesale opportunities
Find buyer of trees
Talk to new owner of lot next door
Find out selling price of two adjacent lots

Things I have learned or rediscovered

1. Stopping outside stimulation, such as TV, music, phone calls, Internet, etc. allows you to focus on what is important.
2. Developing a state of non-thinking can lead to calm and being centered and allows new and/or important thoughts to emerge.
3. You can create a non-thinking state in a variety of ways:
   - Prayer
   - Meditation
   - Visualization
   - Relaxation
   - Give in to the road hum; focus on nothing else
4. If you face up to your purpose or mission, it will show its face to you. (The eye of the tiger)
5. Too much inner dialogue about possible situations is a waste of time and often induces stress.

6. Doing great things requires great focus, great energy and most of all, persistence.
7. You may have all the right ingredients, but if you don't have the right proportions, the cake may not come out right.
8. Finding your purpose is a lot harder than finding something to do. Never confuse the two. Always focus on the purpose first.

As I have been traveling, I have come across several Occupy Movement demonstrations. It happened in Myrtle Beach, Jacksonville, and Orlando. While at Kathy's house, I woke up one morning around 6:15 AM, and tried to go back to sleep. As often happens, my mind engages and keeps me awake for a while. That morning, I was thinking about the Occupy Movement and thought, what would happen if I showed up at one, set up an easel and poster pad and conducted a brainstorming session? I have done dozens of these to brainstorm and solve problems in the business environment. In several hours, we could develop consensus on a set of actions and goals. Come up with something concrete rather than this blather of "we are the 99%," "unfair distribution of wealth".

I find it interesting that this movement could last so long and pop up in so many places and produce nothing of value. I actually drove through Charlotte today to see the downtown and drove right by the Occupy Charlotte group in front of City Hall. For a moment I contemplated parking and walking over to talk to people. But I drove on. Not my mission.

I have been reading *American Sphinx, the Character of Thomas Jefferson,* by Joseph J. Ellis. Jefferson would undoubtedly approve of the Occupy Movement. He favored little intrusion of the government in the affairs of people. His election as our third president was the beginning of the Republican Party, which has continued his voice of no or little governmental intrusion into the lives of citizens.

Paradoxically, the primary complaint of the occupiers is the unequal distribution of wealth in America, which itself stems from lack of governmental interference in free capital markets. So Jefferson would approve of the movement, but be absolutely against any government intervention to right this wrong. Also, being of the Virginia planter community, Jefferson would be in the 1% of his time, the elite who had access to great wealth. Again, paradoxically he was heavily indebted to English and Dutch banks to the extent of having difficulty in keeping ahead of the debt compounding against him.

It is pretty obvious there is no historical underpinning of the principles of democracy and free capital markets in what the Occupy Movement is trying to do. So, there's no historical foundation, no philosophical foundation, and no economic foundation to the movement. It is amazing that it continues. It may just be the smoldering frustrations of the unemployed and disenchanted Americans who have nothing better to do.

Which is a pity, because the movement has captured the media's attention, which gives them a platform for making changes.

Later the same day, I decided to write in my journal again.

8:00 PM I have been staring at this blank page for about ten minutes now. Let's see what happens.

8:10 PM A train whistle blows, pulling me into memories of Erie, where I grew up.

8:19 PM This is another way to induce thinking about nothing!

8:27 PM Why have I spent so much time thinking and dreaming of so many big projects to make this a better world? Is it all just delusions and fantasies or is it driven in a purposeful manner by my life dream? Granted, most of this time is between 10 PM and 2 AM - a time when most people are relaxing or sleeping.

I had a considerable financial cushion from the sale of our Florida condo, Kitty's 401(k) and her life insurance. I have survived for almost seven years, but I have not thrived. The larger ideas cost too much to implement so no progress has been made on them, other than filling yellow tablets with plans to do them. And my daytime activities have only resulted in a Second Hope manuscript that is 90% completed, a Second Hope guidebook and a 15-minute video that I cannot successfully get online. I do have a Christmas tree farm with 2000 trees on it but it is been inadequately maintained. So, some assets have been created, but their time in the light has not been realized.

I have come to forgive myself for my mistakes and my inadequacies of the last six and a half years. The grieving proccss, the aloneness, and the desire to do everything possible for my children, particularly Cooper, have all proved to envelop my attention to the distraction of everything else. So be it. But, it is time to move past all that and reclaim the potential I have felt for as long as I can remember.

I am blessed that the decisions we have made have given me the ability to take this three-month walkabout to figure out what my purpose in life is.

I still fully believe my purpose in life is embodied in all of my plans and projects that comprise the Rich Man plan. But, there is no plan that will finance any of those ideas, other than winning the lottery, which is not a plan. That could still happen, but the odds are against that. So I have to have a firmly executed plan B that can bootstrap me into achieving some of the most significant elements of plan A – Second Hope, M Wind, or One Ocean.

It is difficult to hold so widely disparate approaches to the same desired end result, but I believe I am able to move forward with this cognitive dissonance. Or God could have a plan C for me.

I pull out a small prayer book from my Cursillo workshop in 1981.

My Lord God,
I have no idea where I am going.
I do not see the road ahead of me.
I cannot know for certain where it will land.
Nor do I really know myself, and the fact that I think that
I am following your will does not mean that I am actually
doing so.
But I believe that the desire to please you does in fact
please you.
And I hope that I have that desire in all that I am doing.
I hope that I will never do anything apart from that desire.
And I know that if I do this, you will lead me by the right
road though I may know nothing about it.

Therefore will I trust you always though I may seem to be lost and in the shadow of death.
I will not fear, for you are ever with me, and you will never leave me to face my perils alone.

Thomas Merton
Pilgrims Guide
Cursillo Movement
Diocese of the Erie, PA

9:15 PM

About ten minutes after finishing the prior section, I am struck by the thought of how a personal relationship with a woman fits into my hopes and vision of my future. I have talked with several people along my walkabout about my two relationships over the last two years. But, the reason I am struck about this situation is that a relationship for me now seems very unimportant. I don't yet see how a relationship plays into my future.

It is one thing to hold a general belief that I would like to be in a committed relationship and that I do not like living alone. It is another thing totally to test that belief face to face with a specific woman. Decades ago in graduate school, I realized in studying behavior and motivation, it was very difficult to assess what underlying values and beliefs lead people to act the way they do. So, for the last forty years I have tried not to judge people from their behaviors. I am not certain what yardstick or measuring instruments I should use in evaluating a life partner. I had decided when I first started dating several years ago that I was not going to compare possible partners to my wife.

176

I do know that there are valuable characteristics I would seek in a partner. These include intelligence, personality, sense of humor, honesty, integrity, attractiveness, a spirit of adventure, and their own passion for what is important to them. I suppose that you could assign point values and your own relative ranking of the importance of these variables. But, even for an analytical type like myself, this seems way too outlandish, so I can't go in that direction!

Plus, my own habits and timetables color my view of how someone else would fit in. In looking at a possible partner, at some point, you have to look at the logistics of locations, households, families, etc., which adds another whole layer of complexity to the picture. But, somehow, I have to move forward with the notion of being in a committed relationship and determine how that fits into the larger picture of the new infrastructure I know my life needs.

Of course, being in a personal committed relationship is the ultimate judgment and it only comes about because of incremental decisions along the way on both people's part. In two separate relationships over the last two years, I have enjoyed that progression, yet found myself unwilling or unable to picture either relationship a year ahead at any point. That is a problem when the other person is quite willing to draw that picture! So, for now, this remains a conundrum.

Yet, if I take the position that there are too many other things of greater importance, I will never solve this problem. And I want to solve it.

Tuesday, November 15, 2011

Before I headed east to Raleigh, North Carolina to visit family, I made a few stops in the Charlotte area. The first stop was at a jerky store, the only store I have ever encountered that is solely devoted to all things jerky. They had all different kinds of beef jerky, as well as more exotic varieties like buffalo, elk, wild hog, and ostrich. I loaded up on all varieties, mentally counting them off as Christmas presents for my children and their mates. I would hold a few back for myself as well.

The next stop did not have the uniqueness of the jerky store, but was much more massive and much more revered by millions of fans. The Charlotte Motor Speedway is like the cathedral of NASCAR Racing. It is immense, and much like the Daytona International Speedway, it has its own fervent fans that can tell you precise details of the last race that they saw there. It does not matter if it was one year or fifteen years ago; they still have their story of the last race they saw there. I know because I heard the stories from family, friends, and the guy next to me at a nearby gas station.

I wanted to take a tour of the Speedway, but I would have had to wait for two hours. OK, so now you know I am not a real NASCAR fan (who would have waited even longer). But, the woman at the tour desk said I was welcome to go up in the stands. It is truly a mind-boggling experience to walk out into the stands and be the only person in a place built for more than 100,000 people. I looked down at the racetrack and then turned back to look higher into the stands. Following the rise of the seats towards the bright sky, I actually got dizzy for a moment thinking of climbing to the top. Rather than climb, I sat down and imagined what the race would look like from this seat only ten rows behind the steel protective fence.

The start/finish line was directly in front of me so I put my mind there on a race day. I can see every logo on every car and a few of the faces of the drivers. They rev their engines and the noise is incredible as they move into their allotted places behind the pace car. I watch as the noise recedes only because the cars are roaring down the back straightaway. Coming around the final turn, the pace car pulls into the pits and the roar rises to the ear-splitting level, engines and people competing for volume. The starter waves the green flag and they are off! Drive fast. Turn left. I reach in my pocket for earplugs and realize I left them at home. It's too early to go get a beer and buy earplugs. Wait, it's never too early!

I thanked the tour guide for letting me up into the stands and told her I would come back some day for a race. And, I'll bring my earplugs.

Several miles away from the Speedway is the Backing Up Classics Auto Museum. I had stopped here once before with the family on a trip between our home in Atlanta and my in-laws in Smithfield, NC. It is a small museum, but it has a lot of my favorite classic cars from the fifties and sixties. It also has a small collection of motorcycles. I was delighted to find they had a 250cc Harley Davidson motorcycle from the 60s. It was the exact model I had owned from 1967 to 1970. I had looked for it in a dozen car museums over the years, plus the Harley Davidson museum in Milwaukee, WI, but this was the first time I had found it. Harley Davidson has not made anything this small for several decades. I used my motorcycle to commute to my job as a seventh grade teacher at St. Ann's in Erie. I had attended this school and was their first male teacher ever. This was a strange turn in life to actually replace Sister Vivian, the most feared nun on the East Side of Erie. Occasionally, an excited student who wanted to be called upon would call out, "Sister Crowe!" Change happens slowly in parochial schools.

None of my fellow teachers, all Sisters of St. Joseph, ever asked for a ride on my motorcycle.

Several cars in the museum exhibit had For Sale signs on them. For a mere $28,000, you could own perhaps the best-known car for sale there. It was the racecar that was used in the movie, Talladega Nights: The Ballad of Ricky Bobby. Can you imagine sitting where Ricky Bobby sat? Will Ferrell's depiction of Ricky Bobby has become a cult classic (according to my kids). The producers of the movie contacted the makers of Wonder Bread and told them they wanted to use Wonder Bread as the main sponsor of the racecar in the movie. Contrary to movie industry practice, they were not asking for a product placement fee. Wonder Bread fit so neatly with their story that all they wanted was permission to use the brand name. Of course, Wonder Bread agreed to the deal. What company would turn it down?

Unbeknownst to the movie producers, the company behind Wonder Bread was on shaky ground and heading for bankruptcy. As the movie rolled out to big audiences, the sales of Wonder Bread skyrocketed and it is still widely sold today. Ricky Bobby saves the day! I told this story at Thanksgiving dinner because we have always used Wonder Bread in our Thanksgiving stuffing. I reminded everyone as they gave thanks for all our blessings in life, they should remember to thank Ricky Bobby for our Thanksgiving stuffing!

As I left the car museum, I engaged in conversation with a woman working there. She asked where I was from and I told her my story of my walkabout. Once again, I was peppered with questions and given praise for facing the issue of what to do next. It was obvious she had come up against this same issue, but had not faced it yet.

She was also uncertain she wanted to face it, which is a comment I had heard from several other people.

Several hours later, after traveling on Routes 49, 64 and 1, I pulled onto the beltway around Raleigh to make my way to Burt's house. Burt was married to my cousin, Carol, for about as long as Kitty and I were married. Unfortunately, we lost Carol several years ago after her battle with pulmonary and heart problems (COPD). Burt is still family to me and a great friend as well.

As luck would have it, Carol's Mom, my Aunt Char, was visiting Burt and his family. I told Aunt Char that I was glad that she was one of the few people I had actually seen twice on my walkabout. I had seen her at the beginning and now, very close to the end. It was fitting that the matriarch of my family was part of this process. Char is still energetic and enthusiastic and gives little credence to aging. For her 80th birthday several years ago, her children and their spouses gave her a hot air balloon ride. Shortly after that, they arranged another item on her wish list – a ride in the cab of a semi truck. She still has a few things on the list and serves as an example for my generation of 27 cousins, who are her children, nieces and nephews.

Aunt Char wanted to know what I had learned since the last time I saw her. I told her I had learned a lot about the process of finding out what is important to me. I had learned to empty my mind and wait for something to fill the vacuum. I told her about loving the beach at Myrtle Beach, but realized I would never go there (or anywhere else) to live without knowing anybody or having any family around. She said she was fortunate to have her five remaining children and their families all within an hour of her, but she had just as much fun coming to Raleigh several times a year. Coming to

Raleigh was an event that Burt and Carol's children, Brent and Matt, look forward to. So, they made multiple opportunities to get everyone together. Char felt she knew her grandchildren and great grandchildren in Raleigh as well as the ones close by in Erie, who she would see for several hours at a time, but rarely for a whole day.

Her comparison made me think about my own children and I resolved after I returned from my walkabout to continue the same weekly dinners we shared. It would be too easy to let them slip since Cooper was no longer at home for nine months of the year. My conversation with Aunt Char moved on to other topics, but in the back of my mind I was thinking I should have a more complete answer to her question of "what I had learned."

For three nights at Burt's, I enjoyed conversations with Burt and Char and shared pizza one evening with Matt and Maria and their two children, Ashlyn and Gavin. It was easy to see why Char enjoyed her visits to Raleigh so much. In the daytime, I drove 40 miles east to see my mother-in-law, Dorothy. Kitty's Mom celebrated her 90th birthday last year with a family gathering at our house in Kingston. Since then, she has undergone a few health problems with falls that broke both hips within nine months. Despite going from her own house to a retirement home and shuttling from hospital to a rehabilitation center and back to the retirement home, Dorothy remains upbeat and positive. She has her piano in a community room and occasionally plays for her fellow residents and leads them in sing-alongs.

When I took her out to lunch, she was never ready to go back. So, one day, we were out for four hours, and the next day for seven hours. One day, we stopped at a field of peanuts and I got out to inspect the vines sitting above ground. I knew that peanuts grew below ground, but was unsure if the farmer had pulled them above ground in preparation for harvesting. Just like in the cotton fields, unanswered questions lay all about me.

On the second day, we drove around the Bentonville battlefield from the Civil War. At most stops, she would stay in the car and I would go read the signs and come back and tell her what had happened there. As a Northerner, it is always interesting to see the story from the Confederate viewpoint as they talk about the Northern invaders and how "our brave boys repulsed the aggressors and saved Bentonville from destruction."

I have heard it said that history is written by the victors, which rings true, as every battleground in the South reveals a different side than the history books I studied from.

Friday, November 18, 2011

U.S. Route 1 heads northeast out of Raleigh, directly into Richmond, VA. The road varies from two lanes to three to four in some places. Traffic was never heavy enough at any point for me to make sense of the lane differences. As I reached the Richmond area, I took the bypass Route 288 to the west and traveled Interstate 64 for a few miles to reach Route 522, which heads north to Culpeper, Front Royal, and Winchester, Virginia.

Driving through the small town of Mineral, there was no traffic, but there were a bunch of turns in the road. One of the turns I almost took while looking for Culpeper would have taken me to Bumpass, which is a place I never knew existed. I wonder which syllable you emphasize in Bumpass. Where is the syllable break in Bumpass?

Driving along Route 522, the word that comes to mind is bucolic. There are horse farms, cattle grazing, and various crops growing in the fields, which are mostly harvested by now. Although I have seen these huge round hay bales in many places, I still have not seen the machine that creates them. I am not sure if one machine cuts and rolls the hay or if a combine cuts the hay and a separate baler comes along behind. Thinking back to fourth grade geography, I remember learning that Ohio grew corn, Kansas grew wheat, North Carolina grew tobacco, and so on. But, I don't remember learning much about how any of these crops grew or were harvested and brought to market. There is a story about farms, communities, businesses, and economies that was never taught in school in my day. I'm not sure if that has changed today.

Further along, I see several fields with large round bales that are red or bright orange. I have no idea what kind of product that is. But, I'll bet any school age child living nearby could tell me, whether they learned it at home or in school.

I continued past Winchester on Route 522 and called my friend, Jill, for directions on how to get to her farm from the backside, without going into Berkeley Springs, West Virginia. It involves several gravel roads, but I have done it before. I did have the opportunity to see the sun set four different times behind four different mountains, but managed to get there without mishap.

Saturday, November 19, 2011

I am in Jill's house now in Berkeley Springs. We had a great evening and dinner together. We enjoyed lots of discussion on life, relationships, purpose, and egad, politics. To lighten the mood about politics, I said I was thinking of setting up a website called Boomer Sez. Anytime you went to BoomerSez.com, you would hear the issue of the week. Boomer was going to announce henceforth no more caucuses would be permitted in any state because they discriminated against the working class. Anybody who held a regular job could not fully participate in a caucus because they could not stay for more than an hour. It also discriminates against single parents who may not be able to afford a babysitter.

The website would include several questions around the issue of the week and statistics would update automatically as people voted their opinions. Periodic summaries would be sent to government agencies, politicians, and the Federal Election Commission.

Next week's topic will be No More Superdelegates!

Remember Arlo Guthrie's song, Alice's Restaurant? If we get fifty people a day looking, "then Friends, they may think it's a movement!"

I'm watching a little fan on Jill's woodstove, which is the only source of heat in the house. It is an Eco-fan Original. It has a metal base that heats up from the stove (conduction). Above the base is a six-piece array of more metal. In front of the array is a rotating fan that blows the heat from the base and array (convection) across the room to help distribute the heat. I'll have to check this company out. I told Jill one of my research projects was how to convert unused heat from car engines (or any internal combustion engine) to a usable energy source - electricity.

I am not sure what the round silver knob is between the metal array and the fan. Could it be structural or a solenoid to slowly release stored heat to continue the fan rotation? In any event, a small generator could be placed there to generate electricity, a small simple M Wind device (little turbo) similar to my earlier idea of fans mounted in industrial chimneys to convert expelled heat to electricity.

As I prepared to leave, Jill told me "by trying to make it a better world by your efforts through Second Hope and alternative energy, you are making it a better world."

I replied, "So, by putting out my personal energy, that builds more energy."

Jill then said, "There are lots of us doing that. It's all building up!"

Driving from Jill's house going into the town of Berkeley Springs, I passed a large field with about thirty black cows in it, all with a white earring, which is apparently their identification tag. And as I drove past, I came to the next field, which was connected to the first field through an open gate. And there was one lone black cow down at the end of that field, just standing there looking back towards the herd. So was that a cow that got banished from the herd or one that chose to strike out on its own and is looking back to see if anyone was following him? What does this picture have to do with me?

I stopped in the town of Berkeley Springs to visit Jill's daughter, Happy. Happy runs a small craft and gift store, called Jules. Jules has some unique greeting cards, every fairy figurine ever built, and a small selection of music CDs. I asked her who the woman singing over the background music system was. I had not heard of Eva Cassidy, but knew I wanted to hear more of her music, so I bought multiple copies to give as gifts. Sadly, Eva Cassidy died at an early age and never got to see much of the success her music has attained.

I left Berkeley Springs and headed north through Maryland and then northwest through Pennsylvania to Monroeville, just outside of Pittsburgh. I met my friend, Diana, there to spend several days together and see a Bob Seger concert that night. I am somewhat familiar with Pittsburgh after spending my freshman year of college at Duquesne University, plus multiple visits to my Mom's family over the years. My earliest memories of Pittsburgh include a brown haze in the sky from the steel mill pollution. Most of the steel mills are gone, as well as most of the pollution.

Pittsburgh has reinvented itself several times over the last 40 years and has recently been voted the best place in America to live. It continues to get top ratings for jobs, education, culture, and recreation. PNC Park, the home of the Pittsburgh Pirates, is my son's favorite baseball stadium and is in my top three as well.

The Consol Energy Arena in downtown Pittsburgh is fairly new, easy to get to, and has ample parking. There were several guys selling concert T-shirts in the parking lot and I decided it would be easier to buy one now than wait through a line inside. Just after I made my purchase, a small SUV pulled up next to us and a man jumped out. He demanded to be given the shirts that the man was selling. As Diana and I watched in confusion, a strange melodrama played out in front of us. The security guy (although he had no uniform or badge) frisked the seller and made him unbutton his pants to reveal several shirts stuffed inside. Their verbal interplay led me to believe they had done this dance before. The security guy said, "you have to give me at least one more because my boss is watching on security camera and I need to get more than one from you."

I looked several rows further into the parking lot and saw the same scenario being reenacted between two men. Both security guys returned to the SUV and drove several hundred yards before jumping out and engaging another T-shirt seller. I asked our seller what that was all about and he said it's all part of the game. Security can't arrest them, but they harass them in hopes they will go away.

I was still puzzling over this scenario as we crossed the street and looked for a place to eat before the concert. It was only later that it dawned on me that I had likely bought a counterfeit Bob Seger shirt from someone who was not paying any licensing fee. Sorry about that, Bob, but I'll still wear the shirt.

The arena doors were not scheduled to open for another 45 minutes and we decided to wait and eat inside rather than walk around and try to find a restaurant. The arena seems to be on this concrete island and not well integrated with the neighborhood. My other complaint about the Arena is that it did not use jumbo screens to give you any close-up view of the singer. It definitely sounded like Bob Seger, but all we could see was a figure dressed in black. I was expecting to hear some new songs because the tour was announced as promoting his new album. But, it was only a re-mastered album of his prior songs, not new songs. Had I known that, I would not have been waiting for new songs and the concert would have met all my expectations. What's that saying – Better living through lower expectations?

The day after the concert, we spent some time at a large Christmas festival in Monroeville. This allowed us both to find some Christmas gifts, including some great cutting boards. I generally view shopping as a chore, but I allowed myself to thoroughly enjoy the festival. More than my decision to break out of old habits, I give credit to Diana's exuberance.

Monday, November 21, 2011

I woke up early this morning about 6:45 and dozed off and on until about 8:30. For some reason I started thinking of an earlier idea which was inspired by the Shel Silverstein poem, *Hug-of-War*. This is a perfect example of an old idea that will not go away. The earlier idea was of a game based on a long tug rope that had to be positioned exactly over a set of lines in the center of a floor target. The game required communication to get both teams to pull with the exact same strength.

This morning's idea is a little more complicated. As I began to flesh it out, it reminded me of Jill's phrase she uses in one of her workshops – trust, cooperation, support. Now, this device could be used in a variety of ways, sizes and complexity. It could be used indoors for four to ten people or outdoors (or in a gym or hall) for larger groups.

The idea of the game is to use trust, cooperation, and support to communicate how much tension is required to get the ropes aligned with sensors on the floor target to create the right pattern of equal length of rope on both sides of the target.

There could be auditory or visual signals used to signify alignment of each sensor. The person in the front of the line could call tension adjustments. The person in the back of the line could call rope and line adjustments. Another idea to consider for the sensors other than electric eye or RFID tags is magnetic locks or an inner rod in the rope that has to be rotated in order to align magnets that trigger a success signal.

And the accompanying or built-in timer could be used to allow the group to improve their time. This device could be incorporated into teambuilding courses, like Jill's trust, cooperation and support. Different instructions or array maps could be used to improve teamwork within a department, across departments, across divisions.

Or, a version could be developed that after the center ring in the rope array clicks together, the teams have to rotate in one direction or the other, then realign the ropes with the target map again. When they reach the right alignment, the magnets in the center circle align with the target circle and the target circle is drawn to the rope circle.

These different versions could be used to demonstrate the multiple types of alignment that have to occur between engineering, marketing, manufacturing, and sales to become a successful company or introduce a new product or to achieve profitability. It is easy to see how a package workshop could be customized for different companies.

The focus of this little mental exercise was to convert a game of competition to a game of cooperation. Rather than pull a competing team across a loser's line (or into a mud pit!), the goal is to have cooperating teams align for a common goal. Far too many things happening in American corporations today are based on inappropriate competition within the company. I also frequently see this in personal interactions, i.e., "one-upmanship", and "topper".

What is important to me is not this specific game, which I may never get to use in a training workshop, but the perspective of turning the usual approach to life into an unusual approach. If I want a different life, I have to examine all my old habits and approaches.

11. FOG OF POLITICS

November 21, 2011 Monday

I am driving down Laurel Mountain now on U.S. Route 30, east of Pittsburgh. There is a big lumber truck in front of me. The road has many twists and turns. I am afraid to look to the left because the rain and fog obscure the view. If I look to the right, there is no shoulder to the road, only a ditch with rushing water in it. With no vision and no knowledge of the road ahead of me, I have no thought of passing this truck. So, it is obviously a good time to think about politics!

For many years, I had pondered the incongruities within the American political system. Much has been written about the "fog of war" to explain how things happen or go terribly wrong on a battlefield. There has also been much analysis and heated debate about what is wrong with the American political system, although the term "fog of politics" is not a commonly used term.

But, as I descended the mountain in the "fog of weather," stuck behind a slow-moving truck, I became determined to put my own thoughts to paper when I got off the mountain. So, I made some audio notes on my voice recorder, as the logging truck lumbered down through the uncertain path ahead.

The result of this foggy and dark descent down the mountain eventually led me to formulate the following about my perspective on the American political system.

Why is the American political picture so muddied? Why is every act of Congress passed along strict party lines, with only occasional crossover votes? It is well past George Orwell's 1984, but we now have a Groupspeak mentality in America.

If you don't use the right words of political correctness, you will get lambasted from all sides. Geraldine Ferraro, America's first major party female candidate for Vice-President found this out during the 2008 presidential election. When she saw the polling data that Barack Obama was getting 90-95 percent of the African-American vote, she commented something to the effect that Barack Obama was lucky to be an African-American.

Well, all hell broke loose and she was accused of being a bigot or worse, and she was forced to withdraw from any further public commentary. Anybody who has ever studied statistics would say she made a valid conclusion based on the data. Going further, you would be hard pressed to find a candidate who ever garnered that much support from their major affinity group. John F. Kennedy did not get those numbers of Catholics supporting him. Hillary Clinton never came close to those numbers from women. No white male ever got that percentage of support from other white males of their religious affiliation (or any other affiliation).

Even though every other commentator in America was saying that Obama was going to pull most of the black vote in Chicago, or St. Louis, or Alabama, or wherever, using the word, "lucky," in connection with that was somehow reprehensible. I still can't figure that one out. Of course, there is much more than that that I can't figure out.

Caucuses

Not every voter has an opportunity to participate in a caucus in states that use them. Sure, there may be one within a short driving distance, but not everyone can afford to stay there for two, four, six, or however many hours that it takes. Single parents may have a problem getting a babysitter for an indeterminate amount of time. People who have fixed work hours certainly should not be expected to take a day's vacation to attend a caucus. Caucus rules differ by states. Some states report only the winner, not the actual votes, so if you are not on the winning side, your vote is never acknowledged anywhere. In most countries, this is called disenfranchising voters.

Primaries

There are myriad problems with the present system of primary elections. First and foremost is the traditional pattern of Iowa (a caucus state) and New Hampshire (a voter state) and South Carolina (a voter state) always voting first. These three states represent a small percentage of the voting population, but they have enormous influence over the rest of the primaries. This is because if you are not in the top three after these states, the media no longer pays much attention to you and possible campaign contributors pay even less attention. These three states are not at all representative of America's population in any category – race, religion, ethnic background, or voting tendencies. The next problem with the primary system in America is the long drawn out schedule and the race by states to vote earlier so that their citizens actually have a say in the outcome. In 2008, both the Democratic and Republican National Committees threatened to disallow the seating of half or even all of the delegates sent to the national convention. For states like Michigan and Florida, this meant that any votes from those states would not count. What's the word for that? Ah, right, disenfranchisement. How can a democracy exist where a small band of national leaders can manipulate the vote?

I forget the exact number, but during the 2008 primary, it was estimated that a superdelegate vote had as much impact as the votes of some 11,500 ordinary voters. In other words, the superdelegates could easily control the outcome, rather than the will of the people.

If there were United Nations observers monitoring the 2008 primary elections in America, they could have come to the conclusion that it was not a free and democratic process because caucus states disenfranchise voters; national party organizations changed the numbers of delegates in certain states, and a superdelegate vote counted as much as 11,500 ordinary voters. In other words, America is no longer a democracy.

Information Age

For the last two decades, life in America has been referred to as The Information Age. If this is true, why do we have so little information? During the 2008 primaries, there were thousands of articles written about the various candidates. I may have read fifty or sixty of them and I analyzed five of them. I was looking for the qualifications of the candidates, so I marked these five articles with different colored highlight markers for achievements, experience, policy positions, popularity with labor, gender, or race. I used green for achievements and was surprised to find so few sentences that I could mark green. Each candidate got a few sentences about experiences and all the rest of the articles were about policy positions, and popularity with affinity groups. In other words, it was impossible to assemble a resume for these people who were applying for the most visible job in America.

If any manager can get a two-page resume showing the qualifications of a candidate for a job as an engineer, salesperson, or retail clerk, why can't we get the same information about our presidential candidates? During the 2008 primaries, I asked about thirty people a simple question – What is Barack Obama's single biggest achievement that gives you the confidence he can lead the greatest country on earth? I generally did not know the party affiliations of most of these friends and acquaintances. But, they almost always vote, so I know it has some importance to them. To my surprise, no one had an answer to that question.

Some said he was in the Illinois Legislature for eight years. So, I asked, "OK, what did he accomplish there? Did he improve schools? Help to lower taxes?"

No one could answer the question. Several people said that he was a U.S. Senator, but had no idea what he accomplished before announcing in his second year that he was running for President. Maybe Barack Obama did achieve something as an Illinois state legislator or U.S. Senator that should have given us confidence he was qualified to lead America. But, it was certainly never reported in any of the media that some thirty highly educated voting Americans had access to. Some Information Age we live in!

Huge Turnout

Everybody rightly gives Barack Obama credit for generating tremendous interest in the 2008 election, as evidenced by increased voter registrations and actual voter turnout in both the primary election and the general election. But, when you look at the actual percentages, it turned out that 62 percent of registered voters actually voted, only slightly above the 60 percent that voted during the 2004 election between John Kerry and George W. Bush. That is pretty discouraging; less than two thirds of the people who could vote actually went out and voted. The 2012 election in France had over 80 percent of the electorate vote. Belgium averages over 90 percent voter turnout in general elections. Is America so disheartened by our government that so many people do not care who gets elected?

Lack of hope that anything will be different no matter which man or woman is running the country is certainly part of our low voter participation. But, there are bigger structural elements that have a more significant impact.

Electoral College

The biggest structural element that keeps American people from voting is the Electoral College. America is the only democracy in the world that has this constraint on election by popular vote. I live in Massachusetts, a state that traditionally votes for the Democratic candidate for President. Consequently, many voters of both parties do not bother to vote because they assume the Democratic candidate will get more votes than the Republican, and thus get all the Electoral College votes from our state. So, the election is not really representative of the desires of all the voters in the state. It is more representative of voter expectations. These expectations are fully informed by last minute polls as well as historical trends.

The Electoral College also creates battleground states, where high numbers of electoral votes can be garnered. The battleground states may rotate somewhat depending on incumbents and prior results, but the electoral count is always part of the equation. The natural candidate reaction is to spend more time and money in these battleground states, which gives their citizens a better, more complete perspective on who to vote for. If you are not in a battleground state, you are stuck with reading reports distributed by the various news services.

Another structural element that deters voter turnout is America's different time zones. Voters on the West Coast have often failed to turn out in high numbers because the voter tallies from the earlier time zones have indicated what the final outcome is likely to be. Television networks have become better at restraining predictions until the polls on the west coast have closed, but it is a very transparent process and everybody can still figure out what is happening.

Social Issues

Each election cycle becomes more dominated by social issues. Candidates are forced over and over again to explain in detail their positions on gay rights and abortion, to name the two social issues that have dominated the last two national elections. I find this very puzzling in a national election, since both of these issues are regulated by the state governments, not the national government. The President of the United States has very little control over either of these issues, but every candidate has to spend a lot of time explaining their views, because they know many voters will use these social issues to determine whom they vote for. But, it has little practical implication, and I believe the debate distracts attention from problems that will impact all Americans.

Controlling budget deficits, paying down our national debt, strengthening our economy, lowering energy costs and their impact on the environment, securing our borders, protecting American interests overseas, strengthening our educational systems, and in addition, improving healthcare delivery are problems that impact all Americans. They are problems that the President is directly responsible for. A person's ability to solve these problems should be the defining reason for electing them as President.

Campaign Financing

Whatever happened to public-financed presidential campaigns? This was a great idea that everybody said would level the playing field and help reduce the influence of special interest groups. Leading up to the 2008 election, the leading candidates for their party's nomination pledged to use public financing and accept the constraints that placed on fundraising. But, when it came time to implement those pledges, the leading Democratic candidate changed his position and said he would not use public financing. Barack Obama obviously knew he could raise much more funds from private sources. So, that left the Republican nominee with a significant campaign financing disadvantage.

Viable Third Party

I am not the first person to believe that we will never get past our congressional gridlock without a viable third party. Ross

Perot came closest to success in the 1992 and 1996 elections, garnering some 19% of the vote. Other parties have achieved less dramatic returns and have been accused of throwing the election one way or another by siphoning off votes. I think Ross Perot's campaign came closest to success because it was a multifaceted inclusive effort. Other parties like Libertarians, the Green Party and the Rainbow Party were proponents of a unique, singular viewpoint. So, any viable third party has to find a way to collect people of different viewpoints, different backgrounds, and different interests. In fact, it has to be based on interests, not positions. Democrats and Republicans always operate from positions regardless of what interests should be considered.

Most importantly, a viable third party has to start in Congress, not at the Presidential level. Electing Representatives and Senators is the only way to get traction for a viable third party. There have to be men and women who will argue for doing what is right for their constituents, not what is right for Republicans or Democrats. The needs and interests of many Americans are being ignored by the bipartisan rancor that dominates our national government. All it will take is a few people in Congress to shift the debate to the merits and financing of specific issues, rather than the hardened positions of political parties loath to compromise.

It could take another twenty years before a third party could draw enough interest to actually mount a serious campaign for the Presidency, but building up some representation in Congress would change our political process forever. And it sorely needs changing if America wants to grow and prosper and create a better life for all Americans.

Coming down the backside of the mountain now, with the rain abating and the fog lifting, I am wondering what a third party could stand for.

- Restore fiscal accountability.
- Here's our plan for a balanced budget.
- Here's our plan for paying down the national debt.
- Restore civility in government.
- Restore citizen involvement in government.
- Restore cooperation in the federal government.
- Maybe it ought to be called the Restoration Party

Here is what needs to be done to restore democracy in America:

- The public will finance all campaigns.
- No more private financing.
- No more Super-PACs.
- No one can use their own money to influence the outcome of the national election.
- It is too important to all Americans to be overly influenced by wealthy special interests.
- Ban caucuses.
- Rotate the state primaries in groups. Each group balances representation of the population. Every election cycle, your state is in a different position. Eventually, your state will rotate through the first, middle and last groups.
- The election cycle is five months long.
- No more superdelegates. Each candidate has a total primary vote count. The candidate with the most votes represents their party in the general election.
- No more electoral college. The person with the most votes in the national election is the President.

It is not yet clear to me what, if any, place or role that the foregoing thoughts on the American political system may have in my own personal future. But, at the very least, it may be another example of how an ordinary citizen can think about complex issues when freed from the constraints of daily life and usual thought patterns.

Why Things Matter – Flight 93

As I drove east on the Lincoln Highway that is today Route 30, I stopped at the flight 93 Memorial near Shanksville, PA. It is a somber, sobering place in the middle of a field. Though unfinished, it made a powerful impact on me. Forty innocent people, passengers and crew, died in that field on September 11, 2001. Once they were aware that their plane was being hijacked, the passengers used cell phones and on board Air-Fones and found out that two planes had already hit the World Trade Center.

The crew and passengers huddled in the back of the plane to assess the dire, impossible situation. In less than thirty minutes, they made a plan and made a decision by vote to attack the hijackers and resume control of the flight. The wife of one of the passengers heard the last known words of her husband as the attack began, "Let's roll!"

Unfortunately they did not succeed as the terrorists reacted to the attack and quickly decided to crash the plane. The flight lasted only about six minutes longer after the attack began before the hijackers flew the plane into the ground, killing everyone aboard.

Who knows how many minutes more of the continued attack might have averted this whole tragedy if they had been able to penetrate the cockpit and regain control of the aircraft? Just a terrible, terrible tragedy here. A permanent memorial building will eventually be built once they raise funds for it.

This courageous action to retake the plane likely saved our country from even greater tragedy and turmoil. Later evidence showed that the hijacked plane had a target of the US Capitol building where Congress was in session. These passengers and crew knew from using their cell phones and onboard AirFones that the World Trade Center and Pentagon had already been hit by three other hijacked planes.

Their decision to take action, rather than become helpless victims in the fourth mass murder of the day by terrorists averted the destruction of most of our legislative branch of government. This decision cost them all the highest price – their lives.

I put a comment on the wall where people could post a note.

My comment card read:

> *"Ordinary citizens*
> *Extraordinary Americans*
> *Thank you*
> *Martin Crowe*
> *Kingston, Massachusetts"*

As I drove away from the site, I wondered what would have happened if they had regained control of the plane. Perhaps only minutes or seconds could have made a difference. If the hijackers had held onto their goal for two minutes longer, could the passengers and crew have been successful? Or perhaps a lucky blow of a hard object against the cockpit doorjamb or lock could have allowed a charging passenger or crewmember to breach the door. This was a day that luck did not favor the brave.

Nonetheless, these brave forty people saved hundreds of lives in the very core of our government. Earlier today, I read in the newspaper that the super committee of senators and representatives who form the deficit committee are likely to announce they cannot reach agreement on cutting the deficit, as they were required to do by action of the laws of their own Congress.

So, these twelve leaders of our nation could not agree to take action to save our nation from crippling deficits and financial burdens that our grandchildren and their children will suffer from all their lives. Just as their colleagues failed to do after months of bipartisan bickering. One hundred senators and four hundred thirty-five representatives had many months to agree on a plan to save our nation from ruin. But they took no action.

Most of these people or their predecessors would have died on September 11, 2001 if forty ordinary citizens including two foreigners had not made a plan in thirty minutes to regain control of an aircraft that could forever ruin the lives of all Americans. The bravery of the forty passengers and crew of flight 93 will forever embody the best of America. The cowardice of the 2011 Congress will forever embody the worst of America.

Looking for Light

A light rain began to fall as I wound my way down the hillside from the Flight 93 Memorial. The rain broke up the mist that had swirled around me, but did not stop my eyes from tearing up as I turned east again on Route 30. Darkness soon followed the rain and I decided to get off the back roads and get on the Pennsylvania Turnpike near Everett.

As I drove through the gathering darkness, I could not shake the images of what I envisioned happening during the last terrifying plunge of Flight 93. I briefly thought of putting on some music to lighten my mood. But, I held off, thinking that I had not listened to any music on my walkabout. Wait and see what happens.

I paid attention to the road and the tunnels through the mountains and put my mind into that spot I had been calling the rhythm of the road. I spied a sign for a town called Hopeland, which brought a smile to my face. A few minutes later, I noticed bright lights on the right side of the road ahead of me. A lot of bright, colored lights. I was driving past a huge drive-through display of Christmas lights!

One of my ideas for my Christmas Tree Farm back in Erie was to develop a drive-through display there, similar to one I had seen in Lake Lanier, Georgia, just outside of Atlanta. I was hoping for an exit from the Turnpike, but it took another 15 miles. By now, it was nearing 8 PM and I calculated how late it would be if I backtracked to see the display before resuming my drive to Philadelphia to pick up my son for Thanksgiving.

Then, I realized it did not matter if I got to Philadelphia at 9 PM or 11 PM. Cooper had classes in the morning and I could sleep in. So, I got off the Turnpike near Ephrata and turned back west –yet another backtrack! As I drove through Ephrata, I thought of

Sister Serafina. Sister Serafina was in charge of the nurses at the Redemptorist priests' retirement home in Saratoga Springs, NY, the last place my Uncle Mart had lived. I had lost touch with Sister Serafina since Uncle Mart died in 2007, but had recently heard from my Aunt Char that she was at a Cloister in Ephrata.

I found the Christmas Lights Display near the town of Brickerville. There was a $10 admission donation, plus an extra $5 to go inside and see the train exhibit. I gladly gave the gate attendant a $20 bill. I forget the name of the charity running the site, but told him I did not need any change. The man asked about my Smart car and I told him about my walkabout. Two other young men came out of the shed and joined our conversation. Apparently, they were all bored due to very few cars stopping by during the light rain still falling.

I could tell from their questions that my walkabout intrigued them, as we talked for about ten minutes. Their good luck wishes stayed with me as I entered the first lane of lights. The whole display was not as big as the one in Lake Lanier, but it was well done, with all the usual nutcracker figures, elves, stars, and candles that evoke all our memories of Christmas.

I parked near the barn and went inside to see the train display. Again, I was thinking of my Uncle Mart, who was a big train fan. When he visited us in Atlanta many years ago, we took him to see the Chattanooga Choo Choo in Chattanooga, TN. Nearby was a large model train display that he thoroughly enjoyed. I lost track of how many train sets that Uncle Mart built for various nephews and nieces. This train display was on multiple levels and had at least three trains running.

Another surprise inside the barn was a set of Christmas display windows that came out of Bloomingdale's Department Store in New York City. The display windows looked straight out of the 1920s and 1930s, with animated plywood cutout figures with movable arms. I sat on a bench for several minutes and let the windows take me back to the time when my parents were growing up. A very different time.

I headed back outside to my car and completed the rest of the drive through the lighted displays. There were no other cars, so I took my time and stopped frequently to let my memories of Christmas meld with what my parents had told me about their childhood Christmases. All the elements had been neatly handed down to my own children, with additions along the way.

Filled now with warmth, colored lights and fond memories, I turned to the east again. As I drove back through Ephrata, I looked at building signs for a clue to a Cloister where I might find Sister Serafina. Finding none, I realized it was almost 10 PM, a strange hour to knock on the door of a nunnery. My last memory of Sister Serafina was at the Redemptorist Retirement Center in Saratoga Springs, NY. My Aunt Char, most of her children, and I had come for the memorial service when Uncle Mart passed away.

We were all in the lunch room when my cousin, Tim, walked in the room holding Sister Serafina's hand. He announced, "Ladies and gentlemen, I present to you, Sister Serafina!" With that, she twirled around with his upraised arm and her floor length nun's habit swirled to reveal bright red high heels! She said she had just returned from her native Poland and her friends gave her the high heels as a going-back present. She decided that today was the perfect day to wear them to celebrate life.

Another warm, wonderful memory that made me glad I got off the highway and took a backtrack to find something I apparently needed.

12. Last Night of My Walkabout

Monday, November 21, 2011

This is the last night on the road for my walkabout. Tomorrow afternoon I pick up Cooper and we drive from Villanova back home.

I have mixed feelings about this. I am sad to see this walkabout come to a finish point. It had a few low points as I came to grips with my ongoing sense of loss of Kitty's presence in our lives. As my mind roamed freely, I also encountered a few periods when I was not too happy with my actions over the last six and a half years.

But I found myself no longer trying to justify those or explain my rationale for them. I accept what has happened in any choices I made which were not the best or in fact were outright wrong. I choose now to forgive myself and vow to learn from these mistakes and never repeat them. But the low points are far outweighed by both high points and good points in both number and intensity of value to me.

I am looking at all these notes as field research and will use them, the trip log and the audio recordings to assemble a comprehensive view of the walkabout. This will enable me to develop an action plan to move forward with the purposes of my life.

I already feel very positive about the things that I have learned about myself. The process is just as important as the product. I feel much more in control of my thought processes and have several new techniques to further master (think about nothing, embrace the vacuum, see what gets sucked in).

I no longer have apprehensions about my future. Although uncertainty still exists, I feel better prepared to deal with them and continue moving forward. There are new routines to develop and a new infrastructure to build. It will take time, but I see the cornerstone (be near my kids) and a solid foundation (Second Hope, tree farm, clear the clutter). I also see the same windows to the world that Kitty and I always shared – our extended families of siblings, cousins, and significant friends. Much of what Dorothy, Aunt Char and Kitty always did to let this network know how important they are to us is now in my hands. And I intend to get better at it with Kitty as my role model.

Another solid piece of my foundation is writing. This journal and the process outlined became the foundation for this book. Millions of people each year ask that question – what is my purpose in life? The process in my walkabout can be organized in different ways and timetables. It could be done without travel and in different time blocks.

I do feel very fortunate, blessed, actually, to be able to do this walkabout. Not too many people have the time, resources, and freedom to do this – let alone the skills and courage it takes to face the tiger of your own life.

All the people that I met or knew who I talked with about this expressed admiration and envy of my journey. Without knowing any of the key discoveries I made, or the process steps, or any outcomes, there was a unanimous recognition of the value of the journey I was taking.

Why is it? Why does my mind wander into realms where I can do nothing? Why do my dreams and visions of a better world result in ideas such as M Wind, Second Hope, One Ocean, Community Opportunity Conferences, and a third political party – all of which require large sums of money to see the light of day?

I know that my life dream does drive this type of thinking. But could I have a simple idea I can execute which could then finance the other larger dreams and visions?

I do believe that I am on a path and that God has guided me on this path. But, I must be extraordinarily blind or deaf not to figure out how to keep moving on this path. If it is true that luck is the intersection of readiness and opportunity, I now feel more ready than I ever have and the opportunity is there.

Bring on the luck!

There is an incredible need in America and in the world for bold new actions to reverse the trend of the last two decades to irresponsibility in all walks of life. The projects that I have on my list could help reverse this trend and more importantly serve as an example and inspiration for many others who have the resources to instigate many other changes that we need.

There are probably two dozen foundations in America that have the resources to fund eight to ten community opportunity conference programs for the five years needed to make an impact. This could impact over 200 communities in America, which would be an economic marvel never before seen in America.

So, my ambitious plan for a Community Opportunity Conference five-year program could spawn 200 others! Now, that's leverage! I promise to keep searching for that next step on my path.

My ambivalence about the walkabout ending is overshadowed by the joy of seeing all three of my children very soon! I'll see Cooper tomorrow afternoon and get to drive home with him for seven or eight hours. Then, on Wednesday we both will see Remlee and Steve for the first time in five weeks. Then, on Thursday, Thanksgiving Day, Amber and John will come over and we will all share Thanksgiving dinner together. Gather to remember. Gather to create more memories.

Tuesday, November 22, 2011

King of Prussia 9/11 Memorial

I checked out of the Motel 6 in King of Prussia, PA at 11 AM. I still had three hours to amuse myself before I could pick up my son for the trip home. As I drove past the King of Prussia Mall, I saw a sign for a 9/11 Memorial. About a block from the highway, I found it at the back of a parking lot for the local fire company. It is a small memorial on a raised piece of ground. At the center is a twisted beam of steel from the World Trade Center. Nearby is a small gazebo with several seats. Although it is within a stone's throw of a busy highway and the nation's second largest shopping mall, there is an eerie sense of silence at this moment.

Just like my experience at the Flight 93 Memorial, I feel the world disappear and I stop breathing as I imagine that moment of impact. With my next breath, I realize that I cannot imagine the unimaginable. I pick up a brochure and sit down at the gazebo, but I cannot read it. Perhaps it is the tears welling in my eyes, or perhaps I know that words cannot convey the utter horror of mass murder of innocent civilians.

Gradually, I begin to hear the sounds of traffic behind me. I stand up to leave, but do not know where I am going. I am no longer hungry, so I forget about going to the food court at the Mall. I turn right out of the parking lot and decide to see where this road will take me. Within five minutes, I am in front of a large casino. I drive past without slowing down. Several minutes later, I see a sign for Valley Forge National Park.

I find the visitor's center and learn that a movie will be starting in five minutes. I still feel hollow and disconnected from the rest of the people milling around me. The movie starts and I am immediately pulled into the winter of 1777 and 1778, feeling closer to the soldiers than I do to the people around me. I can imagine what that winter was like, because I know about winter cold, snow, and wind. As I watch, I learn more about the extreme difficulty of obtaining food for all the soldiers on an every-day basis.

Nearby farmers are more prone to sell their crops to the British, who pay in pounds sterling, which is accepted everywhere. Selling to the Americans means accepting script issued by the Continental

Congress, which may be worthless, particularly if America loses the war. So, no matter where their sympathies lie, farmers are forced to make tough choices about how they will pay their own bills and keep their home and lands safe to support their own families. It is well known that not all colonists supported fighting for independence from Great Britain, but the farmer's tough choice to sell to the British or the Continental Army is only one example of the price that freedom carries.

As I walked around the grounds and entered one of the huts that housed the soldiers, I was struck by how the combination of the movie, the museum exhibits and walking around the historic site, made it very easy for me to imagine what it was like during that hard winter. I could almost smell the animals pulling the wagons and see the smoke curling from the chimneys, and feel the cold of a cloudy day. I had very similar experiences in all of the forts I had visited, hearing the shouts of men over the sound of gunfire, and feeling the squish of mud beneath my feet.

With very few clues, I can easily imagine the sights, sounds, and feelings of the past. So, why can't I do the same for the future? I have just as many clues as to what my future could be like, but I find it difficult to place myself clearly there. Other than my mind-stretching exercises playing the If I Were a Rich Man game, I cannot establish any full-sensory connection to the future. What is the missing piece here? What tool am I missing? Am I too complacent because of a lack of urgency?

The 40 passengers and crew of Flight 93 were forced to make a difficult choice in only a very few minutes. They chose to risk their lives to try and save the lives of other Americans, and possibly their own, knowing there was a near zero chance of success. Close to 3000 other civilians at the World Trade Center and the Pentagon had no opportunity to make a choice that day.

There is a line in the song by Janis Joplin, "Me and Bobby McGee." The line is "Freedom's just another word for nothing left to lose." I have never understood what that lyric is supposed to mean. But, thinking of the bravery of the heroes on Flight 93, I'm getting closer...

Tuesday, November 22, 2011

It is 1:30 AM, which officially makes it 11/23/11, which would have been our 45th wedding anniversary. Well, the 2011 walkabout is officially over! I am back home where everything should look and feel familiar, but seems strange. Am I different? Do I look at things differently? Time will tell as I sort through my field notes and try to draw conclusions.

Actually, perhaps the walkabout ended when I showed up at Cooper's dorm room and he and his girlfriend had Dr. Phil on while he was packing. I had not watched television in almost three months except for the last five minutes of the Boston Red Sox season and one football game in Georgia with a friend. The second sign my walkabout was over was when Cooper turned on the radio in the car to listen to music, something I had not done since September 1.

So, where to next? When I wake up, I go grocery shopping for the rest of the Thanksgiving meal. Steve already bought the turkey. Thursday is Thanksgiving. Saturday is Remlee's birthday party here. Sunday, Cooper takes the train back to Villanova.

This is a taste of the old infrastructure, which will apparently come back from time to time. On Monday, I begin to review all of my journal notes, trip logbook, and audiotapes to assemble the new infrastructure to fit the next phase of my life.

I told Cooper on the drive home that I was very confident about facing my future. I was glad I took my walkabout. I feel blessed I was able to do it financially and logistically. The ride home tonight was a miserably long ten hours compared to the last trip to Villanova of six hours and forty-five minutes. But, armed with some new mental techniques, I embraced the rhythm of the road. I told myself we would get home after midnight and I didn't need to know what time it was now.

The rain and traffic which caused a long trip is not an omen or precursor. Those are external factors I have no control over. What is important is what is inside of me and I do have control over that. It's good to be home.

Wednesday, November 30, 2011

In the last week, I have mentally and emotionally committed to writing a book about my walkabout. I have told the kids this and I plan to e-publish it as a good learning experience for doing it with my Second Hope book.

Who knows? It could take off and get picked up by a mainstream publisher. Which can only bode well for Second Hope. With eighty pages of Journal notes, logbook and audio recordings, plus a few shaky notes in my Day Timer, I have a lot of material to work with.

I wrote out a list of twenty steps I needed to complete to write a book on the walkabout.

13. COMMIT TO PURPOSE

A Look in the Rear View Mirror

What brought me here to a new purpose?

Finding your purpose in life at a turning point is not exactly creating a blank slate. All my thoughts about my purpose in life are colored by my past experiences. All of my experiences have shaped my thinking. Every success, every failure has been a learning experience, whether I have viewed it as such or not. Much of what I have done has been forgotten in the maelstrom of keeping the river moving. A lot of what I remember is because of my children. When my oldest daughter, Remlee, was about seven years old, I came out of the house to find her playing at the front of a gravel parking pad in the driveway. I watched for a minute as she was picking up stones, twigs, and leaves out of a rivulet of water rushing off the road from the recent rainstorm. Not detecting any pattern in what was happening, I asked what she was doing. She replied, "I'm keeping the river moving, Pop!"

I have often thought of that joyful claim as I go through the sometimes never-ending tasks involved in life. Shopping for food, cooking, laundry, taking out the trash, cleaning the house, paying bills, getting insurance, car registrations, and all the other minutiae of life can drag you down. So, whenever I feel burdened by these tasks, my mind goes back to Remlee in the driveway and I tell myself, "OK, just keeping the river moving here." The river of life keeps rolling along and part of everyone's purpose is to keep on picking up the stones and twigs that get in the way.

Claiming a new purpose, then, is obviously going to carry some of my past purpose along. But, what parts, and in what proportions? For me, a simple test is a positive answer to the question, "Will my purpose in life make things better for my children, myself, my friends and family, and other people?" A positive answer yields things that will give me satisfaction.

Family

As I look in the rear view mirror to find things that I have done which meet that criteria, far and away, the most important thing that I have done is be a husband and father. The joy of our family history together has given me the greatest satisfaction. In my mind, this is a continuation of the wonderful family life I enjoyed with my parents and four siblings, many aunts, uncles, and cousins. My entire life has been ensconced in the warmth and richness of being surrounded by loving family. While there have been a few times when that tide has been lower than normal, it can always be called back to a higher level.

Friends

The next thing that I see in the rear view mirror is all my friends, some of whom go back half a century. The strongest among them are friends from high school. There are about a dozen of us who keep in somewhat irregular, but continuous contact. About half the group still lives in our hometown, Erie. The other half lives all over the country, but each of us gets back to Erie several times a year and gets together with whoever is around.

After returning from the walkabout, I called Jerry, one of my best friends from high school and asked him that question of who was the "Leader of the Pack." When I told him that Tex and I thought that he was 'spontaneous', he said that I was being kind! He also said, "I was more of an instigator that altered the night's path". He also said that, "We were a Benevolent Society," to which I replied, "A leaderless mob, then!"

So, I am glad to still be a member of our Benevolent Society!

Teacher

I taught junior high school for four years and at the college level for four years. The rewards of inspiring others to learn are incredible. Seeing young people make connections between their learning and their lives gives a sense of accomplishment that your own life has made a difference that others can carry forward. All of my teaching experiences not only made me a better person, but also made me a better parent. My teaching experiences have made me a strong believer that America should have a national service requirement. By the age of twenty-five, every American should have served two years in either the military, government service, non-profit work, or as a teacher. Each of these occupations develops a strong sense of responsibility, teamwork, community, and involvement in making America a better nation.

Trainer

Most of my professional career after teaching has been as a training consultant. I have developed over 200 training programs on everything from sales and marketing to isolation and identification of tuberculosis. My career required me to be a lifelong learner. I worked with experts in technology, medicine, and customer service to learn what others needed in those fields to be successful. The resulting training programs, technical documentation, and job aids have enabled thousands of people to perform their jobs at a higher level of capability. I have also trained dozens of other trainers to design and deliver training programs, which gives me a great sense of having leveraged my talents.

Coach

For over thirty years, I volunteered my time to coach various sports teams that my children were on. Coaching sports that I never played as a kid, like soccer, also meant I kept learning to be a better athlete. Mostly what I learned was that every kid should feel good about what they did on the field or court and every kid should get a chance in every game to shine. Much of my reward was spending quality time with my own kids and making sure they had a positive sports experience. But, I know the other kids had a lot of fun, too. And, oh yes, there is crying in baseball!

Sports Leader

In addition to coaching youth sports, I also served as a leader for several organizations. The first was as President of my daughter's high school Volleyball Booster's Club. I quickly learned that most parents had different hopes and goals for their children's sports experience than their coach did. In addition, the parents had no control over the high school sports system.

In my second youth sports leadership role, I was the president of the Kingston Youth Baseball and Softball League. It took hundreds of hours every year to coordinate schedules, referees, coaches, and fields for a league of over 600 players. It took many hours of a core group of parents to make it all possible. At the same time, I was one of a few people instrumental in creating an umbrella organization, the Kingston Youth Sports Organization, to coordinate the activities of baseball, softball, football, cheerleading, soccer, and lacrosse. All these organizations used to fight over field time and fundraising, but now have a successful vehicle to fully cooperate and make sure all sports thrive and all children in the community have a positive experience in sports.

There is still room for major strides in making sports a better experience for children. Much more work has to be done with the many volunteer parents who have no training in child psychology, positive motivation techniques, or developing teamwork. All too often, they are passing along the same harsh coaching they experienced decades ago.

Yes, there is crying in all sports, Dads. It's part of the learning experience for your kid.

Far too often, we see children dropping out of sports at the age of twelve to fourteen. Part of this is because they have been playing two or three sports year round since they were four years old. The other part is that they have experienced so much negative coaching that as they experience the storm and stress of adolescence, they realize they can reduce their stress level by dropping out of sports altogether. Kids would be better served by being allowed to pick the sports they wanted at a much earlier age. We are failing our youth if we do not fix this problem.

Mirror, Mirror

After looking in the rear view mirror, I feel that much of my life has focused on finding meaning and trying to make this a better world. I was paid to do a lot of the things that I spent my time on, but I also got a lot of psychological income out of my paid jobs, the same as I got from my volunteer work and family life. I always have gravitated towards activities that carry a lot of emotional reward, or psychic income. Several jobs that I had along the way were non-rewarding and became the kind that you hate to wake up for. I replaced those jobs pretty quickly with ones that were more pleasant. So, I never learned to suffer fools gladly, no matter how much the job paid.

One role not yet highlighted is that of writer. In my early career as an academic and then transitioning into the business world, I wrote over fifty articles for publication and presentations for professional conferences. As a trainer and business consultant, the end result was training materials or technical documentation. The written word has always been part of my life and has brought both real income and personal gratification. Searching for the right words to convey the appropriate meaning spills over into personal interaction as well. This sometimes puts me at a disadvantage in a group setting! The conversation may be two topics further down the road while I am still mulling over a great comment someone made.

If what is behind me in the mirror is a guide to what lies ahead, what is the next step?

Resist the Plan

While it may seem odd to step off into the future by resisting the plan or most logical next step, there is some method to this madness. In some earlier writing for improving personal productivity, I wrote about the Law of Complexity. The Law of Complexity states that you must feed the machine and make an issue as complex as possible. You do this because simplicity is never on the front side of the mountain. It is always on the backside. Once you climb the mountain of complexity, you can find simplicity on the backside.

As simplicity emerges, it is possible to move forward with greater speed, which leads me to my next focus for the future.

Be Where You Are

I have learned over the years that it is possible to spend so much time thinking about the past and preparing for the future that you miss the now – the only time we have where we really experience the real world. Once again, a child pointed the way. Many years ago, when I was a busy executive, I arrived home, briefcase in hand, thinking I had to write a training plan after dinner. I greeted my daughter, Remlee, who was about nine years old at the time, with a perfunctory hello and rushed past her. She reached up and grabbed my tie and pulled my face down to hers. She kissed me on the lips, gave me a hug, and said, "That's a proper hello. Now you can go change for dinner."

I dropped my briefcase and went to my knees and gave her a big hug and a thank you. I have often thought of that moment when I find my mind wandering in a group setting, or I realize I am not really paying attention to what someone is saying. Living in the here and now is something I need to do a higher percentage of the time. So, I keep reminding myself – Be where you are.

Keep the River Moving!

The river of life does keep coming at all of us. It should never become the driving force of my day and keep me from a better purpose. Yet, it exists and needs my attention to keep moving. Without taking away the sticks and stones of daily life, the river can easily back up and overwhelm me. This is where my tendency to procrastinate does me the worst. I need to become more efficient at the daily logistics that have to be done and eliminate the ones that are not at all useful.

Persistence Pays Off

I have so many ideas that do not go away. They are written down in dozens of notebooks. I occasionally pull these old ideas out and feed them with either new experiences or new developments that have happened in the world. As I looked recently at several of them, I realized that I had given up on them too soon. Had I applied a little more effort way back when, I could have accomplished them. The Hug of War story I told earlier is a perfect example because I had a client workshop I was developing about ten years ago that could have incorporated that game. I need to get better at sticking with ideas all the way through to implementation.

Once again, I draw on one of my children's examples. Cooper had a tough start to his senior High School soccer season. With fifteen seniors on a very talented team, he stood on the sidelines for the first five matches. I had pretty much given up on seeing him get any playing time. He never complained to anyone, but he continued to work very hard in practice. He was one of the first players on the field and one of the last to leave. In the sixth match, he came on as a sub and played forty-five of the eighty minutes in the match.

After the match, the coach gathered the team together and told them that six players, including Cooper, were the core of the team and the other five spots were up for grabs. So, his perseverance and hard work paid off to become a starter for the rest of the season!

Stick With the Vision

In addition to persistence, staying with a vision can have powerful results. When Amber was a senior in high school, she was the editor of a student literary magazine. The magazine featured poetry, art, graphics, and other samples of creativity. Many of the submissions were a little edgy and pushed the envelope of what was appropriate for a high school magazine. When faculty advisers pushed back on including certain pieces, Amber argued successfully that the ideas and how they were expressed were excellent representations of what teenagers thought about. Sticking with her vision resulted in the magazine winning a national award for excellence.

As I move forward with my vision of what the next phase of my life should be, I need to stick with the vision!

December 5, 2011

Why not choose meaning as the purpose of your life? All the goals I set and tasks I lay out before me are about meaning. All of them are commitments to making this a better world. Face your life squarely. Take the Second Hope Approach to facing serious illness. Cut your own Christmas tree and make it an event your kids will remember in their family traditions. Do something today to clean up the environment. Use less energy and create your own. Treat the oceans well - they bring us life in so many ways.

Reach out to touch others with mail, texts, and emails, phone calls when you are not near enough to actually touch them with a hug, a smile or a kind word and laughter.

Touch your friends. Touch your family. Let them know you love them and will always be there for them.

Speak your mind about injustice. Offer a hand up, not a handout (thank you, Garth Brooks). Celebrate the moments of companionship. Seek them out. Laugh often. Cry when you need to, but not for long. Find the next reason to smile. Never miss a chance to hug your child. Be there for every game, every practice, every dance, everything they let you do with them and for them. You can't fix everything that goes wrong for them, but you can be there to dust them off and say things will get better.

Don't worry about what you get back from others. They can be so distracted by the flow of their own lives that they don't acknowledge your touch. But you know that you touch them. Hold onto that and touch the next person. Just live the life you choose. That is your reward.

AFTERWORD

Over three months, I traveled over 13,000 miles (less than 800 on Interstates) by planes, trains and automobiles, and boats (missed the bus somehow).

Amazingly, I did not listen to any of the music CDs I carefully chose. Just listening to the rhythm of the road, I discovered the ability to think of nothing. Create a vacuum and see what gets sucked in. I stayed in cheap motels, campgrounds, and with a few friends and family who helped me wrestle with my future. Most of the time, I ate in my hotel room or cooked at a campfire, sticking to healthy food, walking almost 150 miles and riding another 35 miles by bicycle. I had a lot of time to think about anything I wanted, old plans interrupted, new plans bursting, opportunities, and constraints. It was strange to focus on myself for so long.

In retrospect, I realize that I sometimes went for days at a time without thinking about my future. I was just engrossed by the present and the freedom to focus on whatever crossed my path that day. It is hard to tell if this was part of the process of emptying my mind, or "creating the vacuum and see what gets sucked in", or if I was merely avoiding dealing with my future. There were several times when I missed out on doing something, like the John Glenn

Museum, because of committing to a certain arrival time. So, balancing "looking ahead" and "living in the moment" will require further work.

Where Am I Now?

It is now October of 2013 and the walkabout book is finished, but I know my walkabout continues on some level. I do have a framework for moving forward with my life, but not necessarily the infrastructure I was seeking. The walkabout was an important step along the way in my ongoing search for meaning and purpose. I am firmly grounded in my life with my children and I am looking forward to the next steps in all their lives. My writing has provided some level of focus and the ongoing efforts to publish my work are becoming part of that, as well.

The 2012 election has further confirmed my beliefs about the changes needed in our political system. I think the actions I suggest are very critical to life in America, since our governing system affects us all in large and small ways. The inaction of the 2011 Congressional deficit committee has moved on beyond the so-called "fiscal cliff" with no significant solution for 2013.

This is a good time to remind myself that it is not easy to re-enter the "real world" and put into practice what I had learned and thought about "on the road." But, the larger ideas I expressed do not go away and the framework provided by what I have learned or rediscovered will help me bridge the gap between today and tomorrow.

I know that there are a lot of Baby Boomers like myself who are at or near retirement who may be asking that question – What is my purpose in life? But, the same question is pertinent for a Gen-Xer, Milleniel, or whatever term is used for any other age group. I also believe that anybody who wants to squarely and directly face up to their future can find his or her own path, whether it is through a travel walkabout or a mental walkabout using these steps:

1. Step outside your normal routine.
2. Turn off the gadgets.
3. Listen to the rhythm of the road (quiet room, beach, etc.).
4. Embrace silence to create a vacuum.
5. Let the mind wander.
6. Seek inspiration.
7. Welcome new ideas.
8. Record to remember.

It is not miles traveled that is important in facing up to a new future. It is the journey through your mind without being distracted that allows you to go where you have never gone before.

And, remember, finding your purpose is a lot harder than finding something to do. Never confuse the two. Always focus on the purpose first.

There are incredible opportunities to live a challenging, successful life. The definition of that is uniquely personal and should not be driven by any definitions imposed upon anyone by someone else. But, it rarely lands in someone's lap. It requires a lot of personal work to tease it out of the array of choices in front of us. I am continually inspired by stories of people starting new businesses or non-profit organizations after they retire. Equally inspiring are the dozens of people I personally know who have taken leadership, volunteering or teaching roles in places like food pantries, arts councils, homeless shelters, marine conservation organizations, senior centers, foreign student exchange organizations, young teacher mentoring, or their local homeowners organization.

Making this a better world has endless entry points. Find one, gather your courage, and step forward. Stay curious and surprises may await you.

Even now, there are a few other surprises lurking in between the lines of my walkabout journal. I'll let you know what I find!

Made in the USA
Lexington, KY
15 November 2013